Nick Vandome

Photoshop Elements 11

in easy steps

For Windows and Mac

In easy steps is an imprint of In Easy Steps Limited
4 Chapel Court · 42 Holly Walk · Leamington Spa
Warwickshire · United Kingdom · CV32 4YS
www.ineasysteps.com

In Easy Steps Limited supports The Forest Stewardship Council (FSC),
the leading international forest certification organisation. All our titles
that are printed on Greenpeace approved FSC certified paper carry the
FSC logo.

MIX
Paper from
responsible sources
FSC® C020837

Printed and bound in the United Kingdom

ISBN 978-1-84078-580-7

Contents

7 Layers 115

8 Text and Drawing Tools 127

9 Artistic Effects 145

1 Introducing Elements

Photoshop Elements *is a digital image editing program that comprehensively spans the gap between very basic programs and professional-level ones. This chapter introduces the various workspaces and modes of Elements and shows how to access and use them.*

About Elements

Photoshop Elements is the offspring of the professional-level image-editing program, Photoshop. Photoshop is somewhat unusual in the world of computer software, in that it is widely accepted as being the best program of its type on the market. If professional designers or photographers are using an image-editing program, it will almost certainly be Photoshop. However, two of the potential drawbacks to Photoshop are its cost (approximately $700 at the time of going to print) and its complexity. This is where Elements comes into its own. Adobe (the maker of Photoshop and Elements) has recognized that the majority of digital imaging users (i.e. the consumer market) want something with the basic power of Photoshop, but with enough user-friendly features to make it easy to use. With the explosion in the digital camera market, a product was needed to meet the needs of a new generation of image editors – and that product is Elements.

Elements contains the same powerful editing/color management tools as the full version of Photoshop and it also includes a number of versatile features for sharing images and for creating artistic projects, such as slide shows, cards, calendars and online photo albums. It also has valuable features, such as the Guided edit and Quick edit modes, where you can quickly apply editing techniques and follow step-by-step processes to achieve a range of creative and artistic effects.

Don't forget

Photoshop Elements can be bought online from Adobe and computer and software sites, or at computer software stores. There are Windows and Mac versions of the program and with Elements 11 these are virtually identical.

Special effects

One of the great things about using Elements with digital images is that it provides numerous fun and creative options for turning mediocre images into eye-catching works of art. This is achieved through a wide variety of guided activities within Guided edit mode.

Advanced features

In addition to user-friendly features, Elements also has an Expert editing mode where you can use a range of advanced features, such as the histogram.

Welcome Screen

When you first open Elements, you will be presented with the Welcome Screen. This offers initial advice about working with Elements and also provides options for accessing the different workspaces. The Welcome Screen appears by default but this can be altered once you become more familiar with Elements.

Welcome Screen functions

1 Options for organizing photos, editing them and using them in a variety of creative ways

2 Click on the **Top features** and **What's new** buttons to find out about certain functions of Elements

3 Click on the **Organizer** button to go to that area

4 Click on the **Photo Editor** button to go to that area

Hot tip

The Welcome Screen can be accessed at any time by selecting **Help > Welcome Screen** from the Photo Editor or Organizer Menu bar.

Photo Editor Workspace

From the Welcome Screen the Photo Editor workspace can be accessed. This is a combination of the work area (where images are opened and edited), menus, toolbars, toolboxes and panels. At first it can seem a little daunting, but Elements has been designed with three different editing modes to give you as many options as possible for editing your photos.

The components of the Photo Editor (Editor) are:

Don't forget

In Elements 11 all of the workspaces have been redesigned to give them a clearer appearance and make navigation easier.

Menu bar   Editor mode buttons   Panels bin

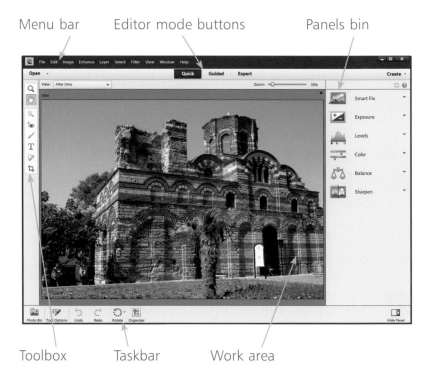

Toolbox   Taskbar   Work area

Editor modes
The three different modes in the Photo Editor are accessed from the buttons at the top of the Elements window. They are:

- **Quick edit mode.** This can be used to perform quick editing options in one step

  Quick

- **Guided edit mode.** This can be used to perform a range of editing techniques in a step-by-step process for each

  Guided

- **Expert edit mode.** This can be used for the ultimate control over the editing process

  Expert

Taskbar and Tool Options

The Taskbar is the group of buttons that is available across all three Editor modes at the bottom left of the Elements window:

One of the options on the Taskbar is the Tool Options. This displays the available options for any tool selected from the Toolbox (different tools are available in each of the different Editor modes). To use this:

 Select a tool and click on the **Tool Options** button to show or hide the Tool Options panel (by default it is visible when a tool is first selected). Other tools within specific sets can also be selected within the Tool Options panel

Project Bin

The Project Bin is another feature that can be accessed from all three Editor modes. The Project Bin enables you to quickly access all of the images that you have open within the Editor. To use the Project Bin:

1 Open two or more images. The most recently-opened one will be the one that is active in the Editor window

2 All open images are shown here in the Project Bin

3 Double-click on an image in the Project Bin to make that the active one for editing

Quick Edit Mode

Quick edit mode contains a number of functions that can be selected from panels and applied to an image, without the need to manually apply all of the commands. To do this:

 In the Editor, click on the **Quick** button

 The currently-active image is displayed within the Quick edit window. This has the standard Taskbar and Photo Bin and a reduced Toolbox. Click here to access the Quick edit panels

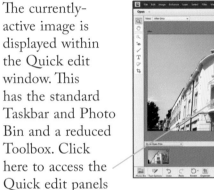

Don't forget

For a more detailed look at Quick edit mode, have a look at Chapter Four.

12

Don't forget

Move the cursor over one of the thumbnails to view a real-time preview of the effect on the open image. Click on one of the thumbnails to apply the effect.

 Select one of the commands to have it applied to the active image. This can be applied either by clicking on one of the thumbnail options or by dragging the appropriate slider at the top of the panel

 Click on the **Hide Panel** button in the bottom right-hand corner to hide the Quick edit panels. Click on the **Show Panel** button to reveal them again

Hide Panel

Show Panel

Guided Edit Mode

Guided edit mode focuses on common tasks for editing digital images and shows you how to perform them with a step-by-step process. To use Guided edit mode:

 1 In the Editor, click on the **Guided** button

2 The currently-active image is displayed within the Guided edit window. This has the standard Taskbar and Photo Bin but only two tools in the Toolbox. The Guided edit options are available in the right-hand panel

3 Select one of the actions that you want to perform. This will take you to a step-by-step process for undertaking the selected action

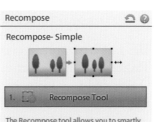

The Recompose tool allows you to smartly re-size an image without losing the most interesting content.

Drag the image handles on the sides or corners to Recompose your photo.

Recompose with finer details:

Don't forget

Guided edit mode is a great place to start if you are new to image editing, or feel unsure about anything to do with it.

Don't forget

The tools in the Guided edit mode Toolbox are the Zoom tool for magnifying an image and the Hand tool for moving around.

Expert Edit Mode

Expert edit mode is where you can take full editing control over you photos. It has a range of powerful editing tools so that you can produce subtle and impressive effects. To use Expert mode:

1 In the Editor, click on the **Expert** button

2 The full range of editing tools is available

Expert mode Toolbox   Open panels

Don't forget

The Organizer can be accessed from any of the Editor modes by clicking on this button on the Taskbar:

Organizer

Taskbar Layout button   Expert mode Panel buttons

The **Layout** button is the one addition on the Taskbar within Expert mode, as opposed to Quick and Guided edit modes. Click on the **Layout** button to access options for display of open photos within the Editor window

The Expert Toolbox

The Toolbox in Expert mode contains tools for applying a wide range of editing techniques. Some of the tools have more than one option. To see if a tool has additional options:

Don't forget

The tools that have additional options are: Marquee, Lasso, Quick Selection, Healing Brush, Type, Smart Brush, Eraser, Brush, Stamp, Shape, Blur and Sponge.

1 Move the cursor over the **Toolbox**. Tools that have additional options appear with a small arrow in the top right-hand corner of their icons. Click on a tool to view the options within the Tool Options panel

The default Toolbox tools are (keyboard shortcut in brackets):

Hot tip

Keyboard shortcuts can be used by pressing the Shift key and the appropriate letter.

	VIEW	
Zoom (Z)		Hand (H)
	SELECT	
Move (V)		Rectangular Marquee (M)
Lasso (L)		Quick Selection (A)
	ENHANCE	
Red Eye Removal (Y)		Spot Healing Brush (J)
Smart Brush (F)		Clone Stamp (S)
Blur (R)		Sponge (O)
	DRAW	
Brush (B)		Eraser (E)
Paint Bucket (K)		Gradient (G)
Color Picker (I)		Custom Shape (U)
Horizontal Type (T)		Pencil (N)
	MODIFY	
Crop (C)		Recompose (W)
Cookie Cutter (Q)		Straighten (K)
	COLOR	
Foreground Color		Background Color

Don't forget

In Elements 11 the Toolbox is docked at the left-hand side of the main window and cannot be moved.

Hot tip

If the Toolbox is not visible, select **Window > Tools** from the Editor Menu bar.

...cont'd

Panels

In Expert edit mode Elements uses panels to group together similar editing functions and provide quick access to certain techniques. The available panels are:

- **Actions.** This can be used to perform automated actions over a group of images at the same time

- **Adjustments.** This can be used to add or make editing changes to adjustment layers in the Layers panel

- **Color Swatches.** This is a panel for selecting colors that can then be applied to parts of an image or elements that have been added to it

- **Effects.** This contains special effects and styles that can be applied to an entire image or a selected part of an image. There are also filters which have their own dialog boxes in which settings can be applied and adjusted. Layer Styles can also be applied to elements within an image

- **Favorites.** This is where favorite graphical elements from the Content panel can be stored and retrieved quickly

- **Graphics.** This contains graphical elements that can be added to images, including backgrounds, frame shapes and text

- **Histogram.** This displays a graph of the tonal range of the colors in an image. It is useful for assessing the overall exposure of an image and it changes as an image is edited

- **History.** This can be used to undo any editing steps that have been performed. Every action is displayed and can be reversed by dragging the slider next to the most recent item

- **Info.** This displays information about an image, or a selected element within it. This includes details about the color in an image or the position of a certain item

- **Layers.** This enables several layers to be included within an image. This can be useful if you want to add elements to an existing image, such as shapes or text

- **Navigator.** This can be used to move around an image and magnify certain areas of it

Hot tip

The panels are located in the Panel Bin, which is at the right of the Editor window. In Expert edit mode this can be collapsed or expanded by selecting **Window > Panel Bin** from the Menu bar.

Working with panels

The default Expert edit mode panels (Layers, Effects, Graphics and Favorites) are located at the right-hand side of the Taskbar. Additional panels can also be accessed from here too. To work with panels in Expert edit mode:

1 Click on one of the panel buttons on the Taskbar to open the related panel

2 If there are additional tabs for a panel click on the tab to view the other options

Hot tip

Click here to access the menu for an open panel.

3 Click on the **More** button to view the rest of the available panels

Beware

Do not have too many panels open at one time. If you do, the screen will become cluttered and it will be difficult to edit images effectively.

4 The additional panels are grouped together. Click on a tab to access the required panel. Click and drag on a tab to move the panel away from the rest of the group

Menu Bar

In the Editor, the Menu bar contains menus that provide all of the functionality for the workings of Elements. Some of these functions can also be achieved through the use of the other components of Elements, such as the Toolbox, the Tool Options panel and the panels. However, the Menu bar is where all of the commands needed for the digital editing process can be accessed in one place.

Menu bar menus

- **File.** This has standard commands for opening, saving and printing images

- **Edit.** This contains commands for undoing previous operations, and standard copy-and-paste techniques

- **Image.** This contains commands for altering the size, shape and position of an image. It also contains more advanced functions, such as changing the color mode of an image

- **Enhance.** This contains commands for editing the color elements of an image. It also contains quick-fix options and commands for creating Photomerge effects such as panoramas and combining exposures

- **Layer.** This contains commands for working with different layers within an image

- **Select.** This contains commands for working with areas that have been selected within an image, with one of the selection tools in the Toolbox

- **Filter.** This contains numerous filters that can be used to apply special effects to an image

- **View.** This contains commands for changing the size at which an image is displayed, and also options for showing or hiding rulers and grid lines

- **Window.** This contains commands for changing the way multiple images are displayed, and also options for displaying the components of Elements

- **Help.** This contains the various Help options

Don't forget

Although the Menu bar menus are all available in each of the Editor modes, some of the menu options are not available in Quick edit or Guided edit mode.

Beware

Elements does not support the CMYK color model for editing digital images. This could be an issue if you use a commercial printer.

Don't forget

The Mac version of Elements also has a Photoshop Elements menu on the Menu bar. This contains the Preferences options.

Preferences

A number of preferences can be set within Elements to determine the way the program operates. It is perfectly acceptable to leave all of the default settings as they are, but as you become more familiar with the program you may want to change some of the preference settings. Preferences can be accessed by selecting **Edit > Preferences** from the Menu bar (**Adobe Photoshop Elements Editor > Preferences** in the Mac version). The available ones are:

- **General.** This contains a variety of options for selecting items, such as shortcut keys

- **Saving Files.** This determines the way Elements saves files

- **Performance.** This determines how Elements allocates memory when processing editing tasks. It also determines how Elements allocates disk space when processing editing tasks (scratch disks). If you require more memory for editing images you can do this by allocating up to four scratch disks on your hard drive. These act as extra areas from which memory can be used during the editing process

- **Display & Cursors.** This determines how cursors operate when certain tools are selected

- **Transparency.** This determines the color, or transparency, of the background on which an open image resides

- **Units & Rulers.** This determines the unit of measurement used by items, such as rulers

- **Guides & Grids.** This determines the color and format of any guides and grids that are used

- **Plug-Ins.** This displays any plug-ins that have been downloaded to enhance image editing with Elements

- **Type.** This determines the way text appears when it is added to images

- **Organize & Share.** These preferences open in the Organizer mode and offer a collection of preferences that are applicable to these functions. These are General, Files, Editing, Camera or Card Reader, Scanner, Keyword Tags and Albums, Sharing, Adobe Partner Services and Media-Analysis

Don't forget

Each preference has its own dialog box in which the specific preference settings can be made.

Don't forget

A scratch disk is an area of temporary storage on the hard drive that can be utilized if the available memory (RAM) has been used up.

Don't forget

Guides and grids can be accessed from the View menu in Editor mode.

Organizer Workspace

The Organizer workspace contains functions for sorting, viewing and finding multiple images. To use the Organizer:

1 In any of the Editor modes, click on the **Organizer** button on the Taskbar

Organizer

The Organizer has four views, accessed from these buttons:

- Media View **Media**
- People View **People**
- Places View **Places**
- Events View **Events**

20

Media View

The Media View displays thumbnails of your photos, and also has functions for sorting and finding images:

Folders and Albums   View buttons   Thumbnails

Organizer Taskbar   Instant Fix and Tag/Info buttons

Click on these buttons to apply image-editing effects to a selected image in Media View, or view the Tags and Information panels.

People View

This view can be used to tag specific people and then view photos with those people in them.

Don't forget

For information about using the Organizer, and its different views, see Chapter Two.

Places View

This view can be used to place photos on a map so that they can be searched for by location.

Events View

This view can be used to group photos according to specific events such as birthdays and vacations.

21

Create Mode

Create mode is where you can release your artistic flair and start designing items such as photo books and photo collages. It can also be used to create slide shows and to put your images onto discs. To use Create mode:

Don't forget

For a more detailed look at Create mode have a look at Chapter Ten.

 In either the Editor or the Organizer, click on the **Create** button

 Select one of the Create projects. Each project has a wizard that takes you through the create process

Create ▾

Photo Prints

Photo Book

Greeting Card

Photo Calendar

Photo Collage

Slide Show

CD Jacket

DVD Jacket

CD/DVD Label

The Create wizard takes you through the process so you can display your photos in a variety of creative ways

Share Mode

Share mode can be used to distribute your images to family and friends in a number of creative ways. To use Share mode:

1 In the Organizer, click on the **Share** button

2 Select one of the Share options, such as sharing to social networking sites, smartphones or the Adobe Revel photo-sharing app

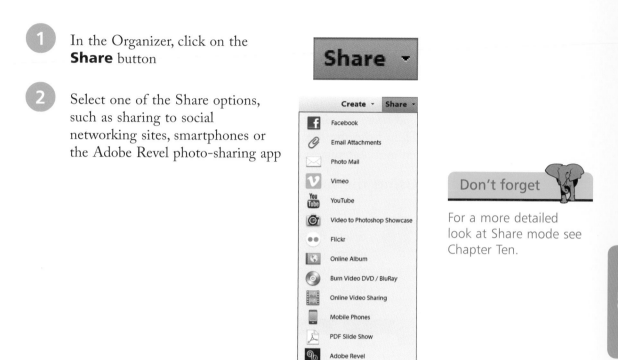

Don't forget

For a more detailed look at Share mode see Chapter Ten.

3 Some of the Share options require registration with an external service, like Adobe Photoshop Showcase, which can be used for online albums and sharing your photos and videos with other people

Getting Help

One of the differences between Elements and the full version of Photoshop is the amount of assistance and guidance offered by each program. Since Photoshop is aimed more at the professional end of the market, the level of help is confined largely to the standard help directory that serves as an online manual. Elements also contains this, but in addition it has the Getting Started option which is designed to take users through the digital image editing process as smoothly as possible. The Getting Started option offers general guidance about digital imaging techniques and there are also help items that can be accessed by selecting Help from the Menu bar. These include online help, information on available plug-ins for Elements, tutorials and support details.

Using the help files

 Select **Photoshop Elements Help** from the **Help** menu and click on an item to display it in the main window. Use the left-hand panel to view the different help categories

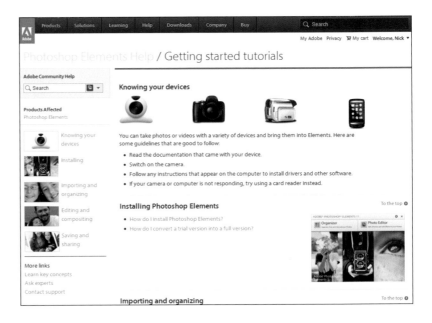

2 Organizing Images

This chapter shows how to download digital images via Elements and then how to view, organize, compare and analyze them, including using the People, Places and Events views. It also shows how you can tag images, so that they are easy to find, and how to search for items according to a variety of criteria such as by keywords, advanced search or even individual objects within the images.

Obtaining Images

One of the first tasks in Elements is to import images so that you can start editing and sharing them. This can be done from a variety of devices, but the process is similar for all of them. To import images into Elements:

Don't forget

For many digital cameras, the Photo Downloader window will appear automatically once the camera is connected to the computer. However, if this does not happen it will have to be accessed manually as shown here.

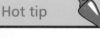

Hot tip

Images can also be imported from existing files and folders on a computer. This means that they will be added to the Organizer's database and you will be able to apply all of its features to the images.

1. Access the **Organizer** by clicking on this button in the Editor

2. Select **File > Get Photos and Videos** from the Menu bar and select the type of device from which you want to load images into Elements, or

From <u>F</u>iles and Folders...	Ctrl+Shift+G
From <u>C</u>amera or Card Reader...	Ctrl+G
From <u>S</u>canner...	Ctrl+U
By S<u>e</u>arching...	

3. Click on the **Import** button and select one of the options for obtaining images

4. If you select **From Camera or Card Reader**, click under **Get Photos from** to select a specific device

5 The images to be downloaded are displayed here, next to the device from which they will be downloaded

6 Click here to select a destination for the selected images and click the **Get Media** button to download them

7 Click on the **Advanced Dialog** button to access additional options for downloading your images. Here you can select specific images so that they are not all downloaded at once

Advanced Dialog

8 Click on the **Get Media** button so that the images are imported. They can then be viewed in the Organizer and opened in the Editor

Get Media

Copying - 72% Completed

From: **E:\<NIKON D70>**
To: C:\Users\Nick\Pictures\2012 07 07

72%

File 2 of 6: Copying File...

DSC_9762.JPG

Minimize   Stop

Media View

The Media View is the function within the Organizer that is used to view, find and sort images. When using the Media View, images have to be actively added to it so it can then catalog them. Once images have been imported, the Media View acts as a window for viewing and sorting your images, no matter where they are located. Media View is the default view when you access the Organizer and can be accessed at any time by clicking on the Media button:

Organizer

Media

28

Folders and Albums   Tag and Info panels

Organizer Taskbar   Instant Fix and Tag/Info buttons

There is a magnification slider on the Taskbar that can be used for changing the size at which images are viewed in the main Media View window:

Accessing images

To access images within the Media View:

 Click on images to select them individually, or as a group

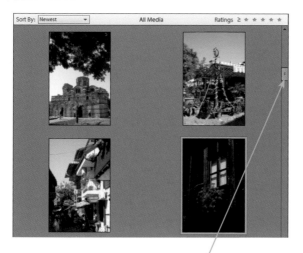

 Drag here to scroll through images within the main window

 Double-click on an image to view it in the whole Media View window

...cont'd

Media View functionality

The Media View has a considerable amount of power and functionality in terms of organizing and editing images within the Organizer. This includes the Taskbar and panels for adding tags to images and viewing information about them:

1 The Taskbar is located at the bottom of the main window and contains buttons for, from left to right, show or hide the Albums and Folders panel, undo the previous action, rotate a selected image, tag faces of people for People View, add images to a map for Places View, add an event to images for Event View, view the selected images in a slide show and access the selected image in the Editor

2 At the right-hand side of the Taskbar, use these buttons to apply editing fixes to a selected image and access the **Tags** and **Information** panels

3 Select an image in the main Media View window and click on this button to apply instant editing fixes to it (without having to move to the Editor)

4 Click on one of the editing functions to apply it to the select image(s)

5 Click on this button to view details of selected images in Media View

Tags/Info

6 Click on the **Information** tab. Click on these arrows to expand each section

Tags	Information
▸ General	
▸ Metadata	
▸ History	

Don't forget

For more details about adding tags to images see pages 44–45.

7 Access the **General** panel to see information about the image name, size, date taken and where it is saved on your computer. You can edit the name and add a caption here

▾ General
Caption: Family vacation in Bulgaria
Name: DSC_9787.JPG
Notes:
Ratings: ✩ ✩ ✩ ✩ ✩
Size: 2.7MB 2000x3008
Date: 9/7/2012 12:29
Location: C:\Users\Nick\Pictures\Bulgaria 2012\
Audio: <none>

8 Access the **Metadata** panel to see detailed information about an image that is added by the camera when it is taken

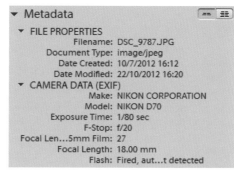
▾ Metadata
▾ FILE PROPERTIES
Filename: DSC_9787.JPG
Document Type: image/jpeg
Date Created: 10/7/2012 16:12
Date Modified: 22/10/2012 16:20
▾ CAMERA DATA (EXIF)
Make: NIKON CORPORATION
Model: NIKON D70
Exposure Time: 1/80 sec
F-Stop: f/20
Focal Len...5mm Film: 27
Focal Length: 18.00 mm
Flash: Fired, aut...t detected

Hot tip

A caption can also be added to an image by selecting it and selecting **Edit > Add Caption** from the Menu bar.

9 Click on this button to view an expanded list of metadata information

10 Access the **History** panel to view the editing history of the image

▾ History
Modified Date: 22/10/2012 16:20
Imported On: 15/10/2012
Imported From: hard disk
Volume Name: Win7

Full Screen Preview

From within the Media View it is possible to view all of your images, or a selection of them, at full screen size. In addition, themes can be added to create an impressive slide show effect. To use the Full Screen Preview:

 In the Media View, select **View > Full Screen** from the Menu bar, or press **F11**

The image is displayed, with the **Quick Edit** and **Quick Organize** panels displayed at the side of the window

The full screen preview toolbar is displayed here

Use these buttons (from left to right) to move to the previous image, play all images as a slide show and move to the next image

Use these buttons (from left to right) to select transitions for a slide show, view the filmstrip of images at the bottom of the window, compare images (see next page), lock images (see next page), access the full screen preview settings, show and hide the Quick Edit panel, show and hide the Quick Organize panel, show and hide the Info panel and exit full screen preview

Theme Film Strip View   Settings   Fix Organize Info Exit

Hot tip

Press **Esc** to return to the Media View from either Full Screen Preview or Full Screen Compare.

Full Screen Compare

In addition to viewing individual images at full screen size, it is also possible to compare two images next to each other. This can be a very useful way of checking the detail of similar images, particularly for items such as focus and lighting. To compare images using Full Screen Compare:

1. Select two images in Media View and access Full Screen Preview as shown on the previous page

2. In Full Screen Preview, click here on the toolbar and select an option for comparing images, either horizontally or vertically

3. Click on the lock button on the toolbar. This enables zooming on both images simultaneously

4. The images are displayed and the zoom command is applied to both of them

Don't forget

Only two images can be compared at the same time in Full Screen Compare. If you select a third image while in Full Screen Compare, this will replace one of the other two images.

33

Hot tip

Full Screen Compare is a good way to compare quality of two similar images.

Auto-Analyzer

Once photos have been imported into the Organizer it is possible to run a function that analyzes several elements relating to the quality of the images. Once this has been done the elements are added as tags to the images. This creates a quick visual guide to the quality of photos, which can be viewed in the Organizer. To use the Auto-Analyzer:

Beware

If you do not make a selection, the Auto-Analyzer will run over all of your photos. Depending on the number of photos, this can take a considerable amount of time.

1 In the Media View, select the images which you want to be analyzed. (If you do not select any images, the Auto-Analyzer will be performed over the whole collection)

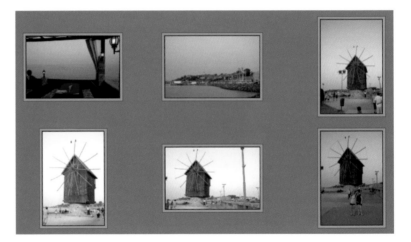

2 Select **File > Run Auto-Analyzer** from the Menu bar. This will then be performed over the selected images (or the whole collection). You are notified once the Auto-Analyzer has finished

Analysis of the files has been Completed

3 The Auto-Analyzer adds Smart Tags to the images, based on the quality of the images

4 To view the tags, double-click on an image

5 The tags that have been added are shown in the Image Tags panel. These are all elements that have been identified by the Auto-Analyzer

Image Tags

Add Custom Keywords	Add

- Medium Quality
- In Focus
- Too Bright

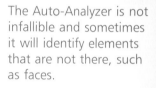

Beware

The Auto-Analyzer is not infallible and sometimes it will identify elements that are not there, such as faces.

6 The tags are automatically added to the Tags panel under Smart Tags. Scroll over a tag and click on the arrow to search for images with a specific tag, as shown on page 47

▼ Smart Tags
- High Quality
- Low Quality
- Medium Quality >
  ▶ Audio
- Blurred

Stacks

Since digital cameras make it quick, easy and cheap to capture dozens, or hundreds, of images on a single memory card it is no surprise that most people are now capturing more images than ever before. One result of this is that it is increasingly tempting to take several shots of the same subject, just to try and capture the perfect image. The one drawback with this is that when it comes to organizing your images on a computer it can become time-consuming to work your way through all of your near-identical shots. The Media View offers a useful solution to this by allowing you to stack similar images, so that you can view a single thumbnail rather than several. To do this:

Beware

You can remove images from a stack by selecting the stack in the Media View and selecting **Edit > Stack > Flatten Stack** from the Menu bar. However, this will remove all of the images, apart from the top one, from the Media View. This does not remove them from your hard drive, although there is an option to do this too, if you wish.

1 Select the images that you want to stack in the Media View

2 Select **Edit > Stack > Stack Selected Photos** from the Menu bar

3 The images are stacked into a single thumbnail and the existence of the stack is indicated by this icon

4 To view all of the stacked images, click here

Don't forget

To revert stacked images to their original state, select the stack and select **Edit > Stack > Unstack Photos** from the Menu bar.

5 Click here to return to all of the photos in the Media View

Version Sets

When working with digital images it is commonplace to create several different versions from a single image. This could be to use one for printing and one for use on the Web, or because there are elements of an image that you want to edit. Instead of losing track of images that have been edited it is possible to create stacked thumbnails of edited images, which are known as version sets. These can include the original image and all of the edited versions. Version sets can be created and added to from the Photo Editor and viewed in Media View. To do this:

1. Open an image in the Photo Editor

2. Make editing changes to the image in either Expert edit mode or Quick edit mode

3. Select **File > Save As** from the Menu bar

4. Check on the **Save in Version Set with Original** box and click **Save**

5. In Media View, the original image and the edited one are grouped together in a stack, and the fact that it is a version set is denoted next to the set

6. To view all of the images in a version set, select the set and select **Edit > Version Set > Expand Items in Version Set** from the Menu bar

Don't forget

The other version set menu options include Flatten Version Set, and Revert to Original. The latter deletes all of the other versions except the original image.

37

People View

People shots are popular in most types of photography. However, this can result in hundreds, or thousands, of photos of different people. In Elements there is a feature that enables you to tag people throughout your collections. This is known as people recognition. To use this:

1 In Media View of the Organizer, either select individual images, or do not select any to have people recognition applied to the whole collection. Click on the **Add People** button on the Taskbar

Add People

2 The Organizer will analyze each photo and display a prompt box for each new face it finds

3 Enter a name in the prompt box. Other similar photos will have this name added to them too

Adding people manually
To add people's names manually:

1 Open a photo at full size in the Media View and click on the **Mark Face** button

Mark Face

2 A prompt box appears on the screen. Drag this over the required face, add a name in the **Who is this?** box and click on the green tick to apply the name

38

Viewing people

To view people who have been tagged with people recognition:

1 Click on the **People** button in the main Organizer window

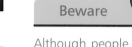

2 The people photos are stacked in a thumbnail. Double-click on the thumbnail to view all of the photos

3 To add more photos with the selected person, click on the **Find More** button on the People View Taskbar

4 When more faces are identified, click in the bottom right-hand corner and select whether they are of the correct person or not

5 Click on the **Save** button

Beware

Although people recognition is very accurate, it may, at times, identify objects that are not faces at all.

Don't forget

People recognition really comes into its own when you have tagged dozens, or hundreds, of photos. You can then view all of the photos containing a specific person.

Places View

One of the most common reasons for taking photos is when people are on vacation in different and new locations. Within the Organizer it is possible to tag photos to specific locations on a map, so that you can quickly view all of your photos from a certain area. To do this:

1 In Media View, select all of the photos from a specific location

2 On the Taskbar, click on the **Add Places** button

3 The Places View window opens with the selected photos in the top panel and a map in the main panel

Hot tip

You can also move around the map by clicking and dragging. You can also zoom in and out by right-clicking on the map and selecting the relevant command.

4 Use these controls to move around the map and zoom in and out on it

5 Drag the photos onto a specific location on the map to tag them at this point. Click here to confirm the action

6 A red flag is placed on the map at the point where the photos were placed. The number of tagged photos is indicated on the flag

7 Click on the **Done** button

8 To view photos that have been placed on a map, click on the **Places** button in the main Organizer window

9 Red arrows indicate all of the locations at which photos have been placed. All photos are shown in the left-hand panel

10 Click on an arrow and click on the **Show Media** button to view the photos just for this location

11 Click on the **Add Places** button to add photos to another location

Beware

If a photo with an existing location is selected and the Add Places button is clicked, the location for the photo can be changed, but it will be removed from the original one.

Events View

Photos in the Organizer can also be allocated to specific events such as family celebrations or overseas trips. This is done with the Events View. To do this:

1 In Media View, select all of the required photos for a specific event

2 On the Taskbar, click on the **Add Event** button

3 In the Add New Event panel, add details including name, start and end date and a description of the event

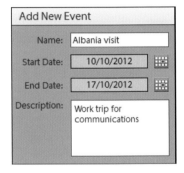

Hot tip

Click on the 'i' icon on the thumbnail in the Events window to see the description for that particular event.

4 Click on the **Done** button

5 To view photos that have been allocated to an event, click on the **Events** button in the main Organizer window

6 All photos for a specific event are grouped together

7 Double-click on the thumbnail to view all of the photos allocated to the event

8 Click on the **Back** button to go back to the thumbnail view in Step 6

9 Click on the **Calendar** to view events from specific dates

Calendar		Clear
All Years ▼		
Jan	Feb	Mar
Apr	May	Jun
Jul	Aug	Sep
Oct	Nov	Dec

10 Click on the **Add Event** button to create another event in Event View. This is done by dragging photos into the media bin and entering the event details as in Step 3

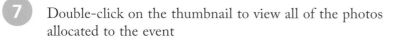

Add Event

Tagging Images

As your digital image collection begins to grow on your computer it is increasingly important to be able to keep track of your images and find the ones you want, when you want them. One way of doing this is by assigning specific tags to images. You can then search for images according to the tags that have been added to them. The tagging function is accessed from the Tags panel within the Media View in the Organizer. To add tags to images:

1 In Media View, click on this button on the Taskbar to show and hide the Tags panel

2 Click here to access the currently-available tags

3 Click here to access sub-categories for a particular category

Hot tip

When you create a new category you can also choose a new icon.

4 Click here to add categories, or sub-categories, of your own choice

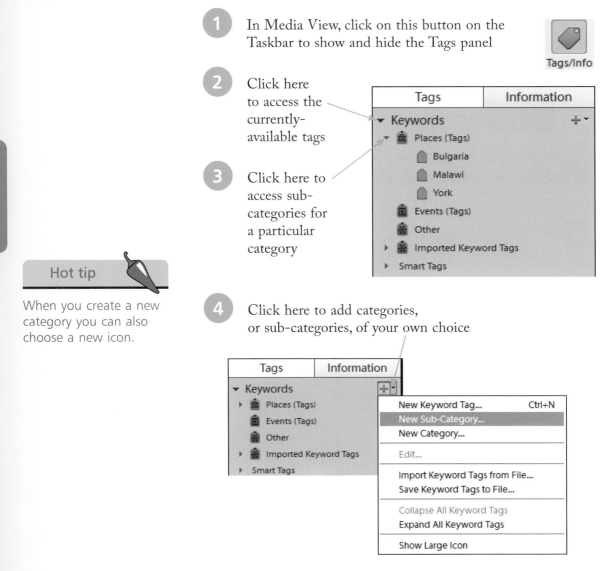

5 Enter a name for the new category, or sub-category, and click on the **OK** button

Multiple tags can be added to the same image. This gives you greater flexibility when searching for images.

6 Select the required images in the Media View

7 Drag a tag onto one of the selected images

8 The tag will apply to all of the selected images. Each individual image will have the tag added to it

Tagged images can still be searched for by using a sub-category tag, even though they are denoted in the Media View by the tag for the main category.

9 The images are tagged with the icon that denotes the main category, rather than the sub-category

45

Searching for Images

Once images have been tagged they can be searched for using their tags. To do this:

Using the Search box

Images can be searched for simply by typing keywords into the Search box at the top of the Organizer, in any view:

1 Click in the Search box

2 Enter a keyword. As you type, suggestions will appear, including items that have been added to People View, Places View and Events View

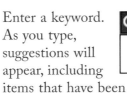

3 Click on one of the results to view all of the tagged images

Don't forget

Click on the **Sort By** box in Step 4 to sort the search results according to Newest, Oldest or Import Batch.

4 Click on the **Back** button to go back to all images

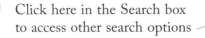

5 Click here in the Search box to access other search options

Advanced Search

Images can also be searched for using keywords within the advanced search mode. To do this:

1 Move the cursor over a keyword until an arrow appears at the right-hand side. Click on the arrow

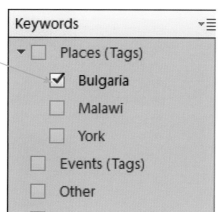

2 The Keywords panels appear at the top of the Media View window. Check on a box to view the images that are tagged with that keyword

3 All matching items for a search are shown together within the Media View window

4 Click on the **Back** button to return to the rest of the images

...cont'd

Multiple searches

Within Advanced Search it is also possible to refine searches for images that have multiple (i.e. two or more) tags attached to them. To do this:

 Add a tag to an image, or images

 Add another tag to the image, or images, so that there are at least two attached

3 In the Advanced Search panel, check on one of the search tags. This will show all of the images that have this tag

4 To refine the search, check on another tag. This will show only the images that have both of these tags attached to them

48

Searching by objects

In Elements it is also possible to search for images based on specific objects. For instance, you can search for images with a particular building, landscape or animal. To do this:

 Click on an image that contains the object that you want to use for the search criteria

 Click on the down arrow next to the Search box and select the **Object Search** option

Drag the markers of the box over the object to resize it, or click and drag inside it to move the whole box

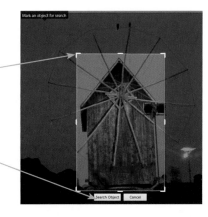

Click on the **Search Object** button

Images with similar objects are displayed, with a percentage rating of how close the object match is

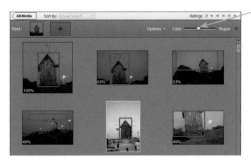

49

Albums

Albums in Elements are similar to physical photo albums: they are a location into which you can store all of your favorite groups of images. Once they have been stored there they can easily be found when required. To create albums:

1 In the Media View, click here in the Albums panel and select **New Album**

2 Enter a name for the new album

3 Select the images that you would like included in the new album and drag them into the Content panel

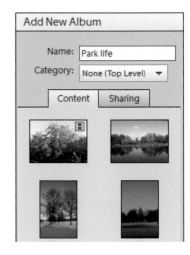

4 Click on the **OK** button

5 The selected images are placed into the new album. Click on an album to view the images within it

Folders

One important factor in storing and searching for photos is the use of folders. Elements can replicate the folder structure that you have on your hard drive and also create new folders and edit existing ones. To work with folders in Elements:

1 The available folders are listed below the Albums section. Click on a folder to view its contents

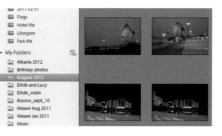

2 New folders are created whenever you import photos into Elements using the **Import > From Files and Folders** command

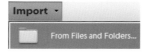

3 Click on this button to view the folder hierarchy as it is on your hard drive

Folders
- My Pictures
  - My Videos
- Computer
  - A:
  - C:
    - ProgramData
    - Users
      - Nick
        - Pictures
          - Albania 2012
          - Birthday photos
          - Bulgaria 2012
          - Eilidh and Lucy
          - Eilidh_violin
          - Kosovo_sept_10
          - Malawi Aug 2011
          - Malawi Jan 2011
          - Olympic Torch
          - Perth Winter
          - Wildlife 2012

4 In hierarchy view, right-click on a folder to access the available options for editing it or adding a new folder

- Reveal in Explorer
- Add to Watched Folders
- Import Media
- New Folder
- Rename Folder
- Delete Folder
- Create an Instant Album
- Show All SubFolders

Opening and Saving Images

Once you have captured images with a digital camera, or a scanner, and stored them on your computer, you can open them in any of the Editor modes. There are a number of options for this:

Open command

1 Select **File > Open** from the Menu bar or click on the **Open** button and select an option

2 Select an image from your hard drive and click **Open**

Open As command
This can be used to open a file in a different file format from its original format. To do this:

1 Select **File > Open As** from the Menu bar

2 Select an image and select the file format. Click **Open**

Saving images
When saving digital images, it is always a good idea to save them in at least two different file formats, particularly if layered objects, such as text and shapes, have been added. One of these formats should be the proprietary Photoshop format PSD or PDD. The reason for using this is that it will retain all of the layered information within an image. So, if a text layer has been added, it will still be available for editing, once it has been saved and closed.

The other format that an image should be saved in, is the one most appropriate for the use to which it is going to be put. Therefore, images that are going to be used on the Web should be saved as JPEG, GIF or PNG files, while an image that is going to be used for printing should be saved in another format, such as TIFF. Once images have been saved in these formats, all of the layered information within them becomes flattened into a single layer and it will not be possible to edit this.

Working with Video

As well as using Elements for viewing and organizing photos, it can also be used in the same way with video. Video can be imported into Elements in a number of ways:

- From a camera that has video recording capabilities

- From a digital video camera

- From a cell/mobile phone

- From video that has been created in the Elements Premiere program. This is a companion program to Elements and is used to manipulate and edit video. It can be bought in a package with Elements, or individually. For more details see *www.adobe.com/products/premiere-elements/*

To download video into Elements:

Don't forget

Elements Premiere can be bought as a package with Elements, or it can be bought individually.

1 Connect the device containing the video. In the Organizer, click on the **Import** button, select the required device and download in the same way as for photos

2 The video is downloaded and displayed in the Organizer in the same way as photos

Beware

Video files are usually much larger in size than photos, and if you have lots of them they will take up a lot of space on your computer.

3 Video clips are identified by this symbol on their thumbnail in Media View in the Organizer

...cont'd

Viewing video
To view video clips:

 Double-click on the clip in the Media View. The Elements video player will open and play the video clip

 Use the controls underneath the video window to navigate through the clip and adjust the volume

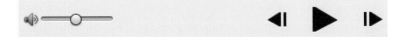

Don't forget

The **Find > By Media Type** option can also be used to find audio files, projects and PDFs.

Finding video
To find video clips within Elements:

 In the Organizer, select **Find > By Media Type > Video** from the Menu bar

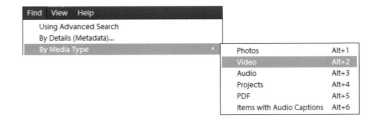

3 First Digital Steps

This chapter shows how to get up and running with digital image editing, and details some effective editing techniques for improving digital images, such as improving the overall color, removing unwanted items and changing the size and shape of images.

Color Enhancements

Some of the simplest, but most effective, editing changes that can be made to digital images are color enhancements. These can help to transform a mundane image into a stunning one, and Elements offers a variety of methods for achieving this. Some of these are verging towards the professional end of image editing, while others are done almost automatically by Elements. These are known as Auto adjustments and some simple manual adjustments can also be made to the brightness and contrast of an image. All of these color enhancement features can be accessed from the Enhance menu on the Menu bar in Expert and Quick edit modes.

Auto Levels
This automatically adjusts the overall color tone in an image in relation to the lightest and darkest points in the image:

Auto Contrast
This automatically adjusts the contrast in an image:

Auto Color Correction

This automatically adjusts all the color elements within an image:

Adjust Brightness/Contrast

This can be used to manually adjust the brightness and contrast in an image:

 Select **Enhance > Adjust Lighting > Brightness/Contrast** from the Menu bar (in either Expert or Quick edit mode)

 Drag the sliders to adjust the image brightness and contrast

3 Click on the **OK** button

4 The brightness and contrast (and a range of other color editing functions) can also be adjusted using the panels in Quick edit mode

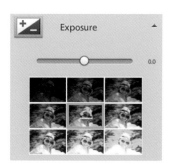

Don't forget

Apply small amounts of Brightness and Contrast at a time when you are editing an image. This will help ensure that the end result does not look too unnatural.

57

Hot tip

Always make sure that the Preview box is checked when you are applying color enhancements. This will display the changes as you make them and before they are applied to the image.

...cont'd

Adjust Shadows/Highlights

One problem that most photographers encounter at some point, is where part of an image is exposed correctly while another part is either over- or under-exposed. If this is corrected using general color correction techniques, such as levels or brightness and contrast, the poorly-exposed area may be improved, but at the expense of the area that was correctly exposed initially.

To overcome this, the Shadows/Highlights command can be used to adjust particular tonal areas of an image. To do this:

1 Open an image where one part is correctly exposed and another part is incorrectly exposed

2 Select **Enhance > Adjust Lighting > Shadows/ Highlights** from the Menu bar

3 Make the required adjustments by dragging the sliders

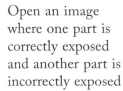

4 Click on the **OK** button

5 The poorly-exposed areas of the image have been corrected, without altering the rest of the properly-exposed image

Cropping

Cropping is a technique that can be used to remove unwanted areas of an image and highlight the main subject. The area to be cropped can only be selected as a rectangle. To crop an image:

 Select the **Crop** tool from the Toolbox

2 Click and drag on an image to select the area to be cropped. The area that is selected is retained and the area to be cropped appears grayed-out

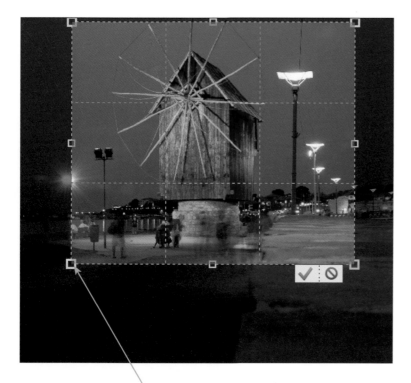

Hot tip

The Tool Options for the Crop tool has an option for selecting pre-set sizes for the crop tool. This results in the crop being in specific proportions. For instance, if you want to print an image at 10 x 8 size, you can use this pre-set crop size to ensure that the cropped image has the correct proportions. The image dialog box will also be updated accordingly.

3 Click and drag on these markers to resize the crop area

4 Click on the check mark to accept the changes, or the circle to reject them

...cont'd

Overlay crop options

When performing cropping it is also possible to use various overlay grids to help the composition of the image. One of these is the Rule of Thirds. This is a photographic technique where a nine-segment grid is used to position elements within the image. Generally, the items that you want to give the most prominence to should be positioned at one of the intersections of the lines. To use the Rule of Thirds grid:

 Don't forget

The different crop options are all accessed from the Tool Options panel, with the Crop tool selected.

1 Select the **Crop** tool and click on the **Rule of Thirds** button in the Tool Options panel

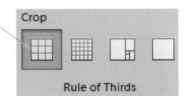

2 Crop the image so that at least one of the main subjects is located at the intersections of the lines in grid. This can be in the foreground or the background

3 The image is cropped according to the Rule of Thirds grid

Images can also be cropped using a larger grid. This can be useful if you are trying to align items within an image:

Another overlay option is the **Golden Ratio**. This is based on a complicated mathematical formula that is thought to create the most aesthetically pleasing ratio in terms of where a main subject appears. If the Golden Ratio overlay is used, the main subject should appear at the point of the dot in the overlay:

Don't forget

Although the Golden Ratio is a mathematical equation based on the ratio of quantities, it has been adopted by artists and architects for hundreds of years due to its perceived aesthetic qualities and appeal.

Cloning

Cloning is a technique that can be used to copy one area of an image over another. This can be used to cover up small imperfections in an image, such as a dust mark or a spot, and also to copy or remove large items in an image, such as a person.

To clone items:

1 Select the **Clone Stamp** tool from the Toolbox

2 Set the Clone Stamp options in the Tool Options panel

3 Hold down Alt and click on the image to select a source point from which the cloning will start

4 Drag the cursor to copy everything over which the selection point marker passes

Pattern Cloning

The Pattern Stamp tool can be used to copy a selected pattern over an image, or a selected area of an image. To do this:

1 Select the **Pattern Stamp** tool from the Toolbox

2 Click here in the Tool Options panel to access the available patterns

3 Select a pattern for the Pattern Stamp tool

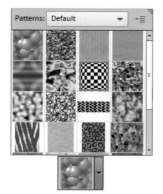

4 Click and drag on an image to copy the selected pattern over it

Healing Brush

One of the favorite techniques in digital imaging is removing unwanted items, particularly physical blemishes, such as spots and wrinkles. This can be done with the Clone tool but the effects can sometimes be too harsh, as a single area is copied over the affected item. A more subtle effect can be achieved with the Healing Brush and the Spot Healing Brush tools. The Healing Brush can be used to remove blemishes over larger areas, such as wrinkles:

1 Open an image with blemishes covering a reasonably large area, i.e. more than a single spot

2 Select the **Healing Brush** tool from the Toolbox and make the required selections in the Tool Options panel

3 Hold down **Alt** and click on an area of the image to load the Healing Brush tool. Drag over the affected area. The cross is the area which is copied beneath the circle. At this point the overall tone is not perfect and looks too pink

4 Release the mouse and the Healing Brush blends the affected area with the one that was copied over it. This creates a much more natural skin tone

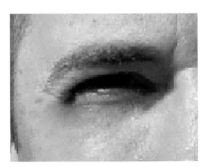

Spot Healing Brush

The Spot Healing Brush is very effective for quickly removing small blemishes in an image, such as spots. To do this:

 1 Open an image and zoom in on the area with the blemish

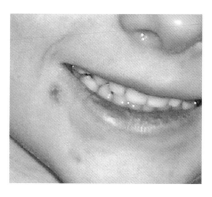

Hot tip

When dragging over a blemish with the Spot Healing Brush tool, make sure the brush size is larger than the area of the blemish. This will ensure that you can cover the blemish in a single stroke.

2 Select the **Spot Healing Brush** tool from the Toolbox and make the required selections in the Tool Options panel

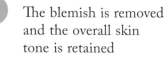

3 Drag the Spot Healing Brush tool over the affected area

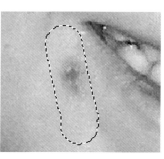

4 The blemish is removed and the overall skin tone is retained

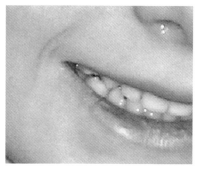

Uncluttering a Photo

As well as using the Healing Brush to remove small blemishes, it can also be used to remove larger objects in the foreground or background of an image. This can be a very effective way to unclutter a photo. To do this:

Hot tip

If you master the technique of using the Healing Brush to remove unwanted items you can utilize this when taking photos: if there are objects in the way you can still take the photo, confident that you can remove them later on.

1 Open the image with the objects that you want to remove

2 Select the **Healing Brush** tool

3 Select the brush size for the Healing Brush. This can be quite large if it is a fairly uniformed area that will be copied

4 Hold down **Alt** and click on an area that you want to use to copy over the object you want to remove

5 Drag the Healing Brush tool over the objects you want to remove. This will then be blended with the area selected in Step 4

6 The unwanted object(s) are removed from the photo. This is effective for either the foreground or the background of the photo. In some cases the Healing Brush tool may need to be loaded from different locations to blend the different areas of the photo as accurately as possible

Rotating

Various rotation commands can be applied to images, and also individual layers in layered images. This can be useful for positioning items and also for correcting the orientation of an image that is on its side or upside down.

Rotating a whole image

1 Select **Image > Rotate** from the Menu bar

2 Select a rotation option from the menu

3 Select **Custom** to enter your own value for the amount you want an image rotated

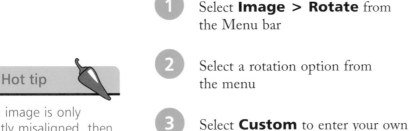

90° Left
90° Right
180°
Custom...
Flip Horizontal
Flip Vertical

Free Rotate Layer
Rotate Layer 90° Left
Rotate Layer 90° Right
Rotate Layer 180°
Flip Layer Horizontal
Flip Layer Vertical

Straighten and Crop Image
Straighten Image

Rotate Canvas

Angle: 5 ● °Ri... ○ °L...

OK
Cancel

4 Click on the **OK** button

OK

Rotating a layer

To rotate separate layers within an image:

1 Open an image that consists of two or more layers. Select one of the layers in the Layers panel

2 Select **Image > Rotate** from the Menu bar

3 Select a layer rotation option from the menu

4 The selected layer is rotated independently

Transforming

The Transform commands can be used to resize an image, and to apply some basic distortion techniques. These commands can be accessed by selecting **Image > Transform** from the Menu bar.

Free Transform
This enables you to manually alter the size and shape of an image. To do this:

 Select **Image > Transform > Free Transform** from the Menu bar

 Click and drag here to transform the vertical and horizontal size of the image. Hold down **Shift** to transform it in proportion

Don't forget

The other options from the Transform menu are Skew, Distort and Perspective. These can be accessed and applied in a similar way to the Free Transform option.

69

Magnification

There are a number of ways in Elements in which the magnification at which an image is being viewed can be increased or decreased. This can be useful if you want to zoom in on a particular part of an image, for editing purposes, or if you want to view a whole image to see the result of editing effects that have been applied.

View menu

 Select **View** from the Menu bar and select one of the options from the View menu

View	Window	Help
New Window for bulgaria4.jpg		
Zoom In		Ctrl+=
Zoom Out		Ctrl+-
Fit on Screen		Ctrl+0
Actual Pixels		Ctrl+1
Print Size		
Selection		Ctrl+H
Rulers		Shift+Ctrl+R
Grid		Ctrl+'

Zoom tool

 Select the **Zoom** tool from the Toolbox

Click once on an image to enlarge it (usually by 100% each time). Hold down **Alt** and click to decrease the magnification

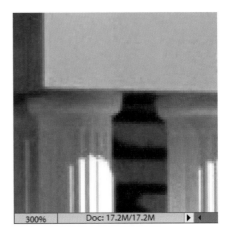

300%   Doc: 17.2M/17.2M

Navigator panel

This can be used to move around an image and also magnify certain areas. To use the Navigator panel:

1 Access the **Navigator** panel by selecting **Window > Navigator** from the Menu bar

2 Drag this slider to magnify the area of the image within the red rectangle

71

3 Drag the rectangle to change the area of the image that is being magnified

Eraser

The Eraser tool can be used to remove areas of an image. In a simple, single layer image, this can just leave a blank hole, which has to be filled with something. The Eraser options are:

Don't forget

The Background Eraser tool can be used to remove an uneven background. To do this, drag over the background with the Background Eraser tool and, depending on the settings in the Tool Options panel, everything that it is dragged over will be removed.

1. **Eraser**, which can be used to erase part of the background image or a layer within it

2. **Background Eraser**, which can be used to remove an uneven background

3. **Magic Eraser**, which can be used to quickly remove a solid background (see below)

Erasing a background

With the Magic Eraser tool, it is possible to delete a colored background in an image. To do this:

Don't forget

If the Contiguous box is not checked, the background color will be removed wherever it occurs in the image. If the Contiguous box is checked, the background color will only be removed where it touches another area of the same color, which is not broken by another element of the image.

1. Open an image with an evenly-colored background

2. Select the **Magic Eraser** and make the required selections in the Tool Options panel. Make sure the Contiguous box is not checked

3. Click once on the background. It is removed from the image, regardless of where it occurs

4 Quick Wins

This chapter looks at some of the "quick wins" that can be done in Elements and also shows some of the Guided and Quick edit options.

Removing Red-eye

One of the most common problems with photographs of people, whether they are taken digitally or with a film-based camera, is red-eye. This is caused when the camera's flash is used and then reflects in the subject's pupils. This can create the dreaded red-eye effect, when the subject can unintentionally be transformed into a demonic character. Unless you have access to professional studio lighting equipment, or have a removable flash unit that can be positioned away from the subject's face, sooner or later you will capture images that contain red-eye.

Elements has recognized that removing red-eye is one of the top priorities for most amateur photographers and a specific tool for this purpose has been included in the Toolbox: the Red Eye Removal tool. This is available in Expert or Quick edit modes:

Hot tip

The best way to deal with red-eye is to avoid it in the first place. Try using a camera that has a red-eye reduction function. This uses an extra flash, just before the picture is taken, to diminish the effect of red-eye.

Hot tip

In Guided edit mode, the Perfect Portrait option also has a red-eye removal function.

1 Open an image that contains red-eye

2 Select the **Zoom** tool from the Toolbox

3 Drag around the affected area until it appears at a suitable magnification

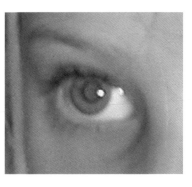

Hot tip

Red-eye can be removed automatically by clicking on the **Auto Correct** button in the Red Eye Removal Tool Options panel.

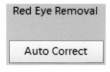

4 Select the **Red Eye Removal** tool from the Toolbox

5 Click in the Tool Options panel to select the size of the pupil and the amount by which it will be darkened

6 Click once on the red-eye, or drag around the affected area

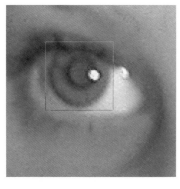

Hot tip

Red-eye can also be removed when images are being downloaded from the camera. This is an option in the Photo Downloader window.

7 The red-eye is removed

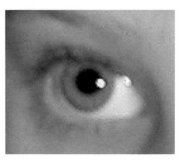

Changing to Black and White

Most digital cameras and scanners are capable of converting color images into black and white at the point of capture. However, it is also possible to use Elements to convert existing color images into black and white ones. To do this:

1 Open a color image and select **Enhance > Convert to Black and White** from the Menu bar

2 The Convert to Black and White dialog box has various options for how the image is converted

Convert to Black and White

OK
Cancel
Reset

Before

After

Tip

Select a style of black and white conversion. Each style uses a different amount of the red, green, and blue color channels of the original image to produce a specific look. Make further adjustments by moving the sliders below. Learn more about: Convert to Black and White

Undo
Redo

Select a style:

Infrared Effect
Newspaper
Portraits
Scenic Landscape
Urban/Snapshots
Vivid Landscapes

Adjust Intensity:

Red:
Green:
Blue:
Contrast:

3 Select the type of black and white effect to be applied, depending on the subject in the image

Select a style:

Infrared Effect
Newspaper
Portraits
Scenic Landscape
Urban/Snapshots
Vivid Landscapes

4 Drag these sliders to specify the intensity of the effect to be applied for different elements

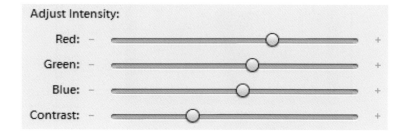

Adjust Intensity:

Red: – +
Green: – +
Blue: – +
Contrast: – +

5 Click on the **OK** button

OK

6 The image is converted into black and white, according to the settings that have been selected

Hot tip

A similar effect can be achieved by selecting **Enhance > Adjust Color > Remove Color** from the Menu bar.

Quick Edit Mode Options

The Quick edit options in Elements offer a number of functions within the one location. This makes it easier to apply a number of techniques at the same time.

Using Quick edit mode

 Open an image in the Editor and click on the **Quick** button

 The Quick edit mode has a modified Toolbox, with fewer tools, that is displayed here

 Quick edit mode correction panels are located here

Select one of the correction panels and click on a thumbnail to apply the effect to the active image

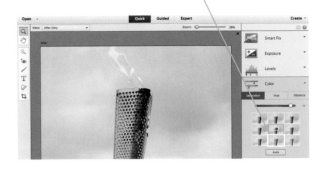

Whitening teeth

One of the tool options in the Quick edit mode Toolbox is for whitening teeth in a photo. To do this:

1 Open an image and click on the **Whiten Teeth** tool

2 Click on the **Zoom** tool

3 Drag the Zoom tool around the teeth area
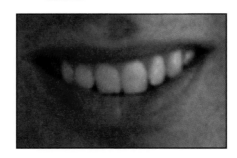

Don't forget

The other tools in the Quick edit mode Toolbox are Zoom, Hand, Quick Selection, Red Eye Removal, Text, Healing Brush and Crop.

79

4 Click here to select a brush size for the Whiten Teeth tool
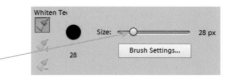

5 Drag the Whiten Teeth tool over the teeth
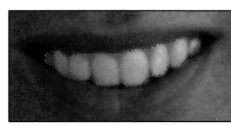

6 The teeth area is selected and whitened in one operation

...cont'd

Smart Fix panel

This performs several editing changes in a single operation. Click on the Auto button to have the changes applied automatically, or drag the slider to specify the amount of the editing changes. Click on the thumbnails to apply preset amounts of the change.

Don't forget

Changes are displayed in the main Quick edit window as they are being made.

Exposure panel

This provides options for adjusting the lighting and contrast in an image. Drag the sliders to adjust the exposure or click on one of the thumbnails to apply a preset option.

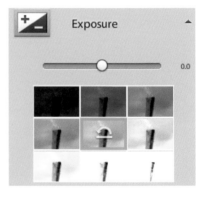

Levels panel

This provides options for adjusting the lightest and darkest points in an image. This is done by adjusting the shadows, midtones and highlights in an image. Drag the slider to adjust this or click on one of the thumbnails for an auto option.

Color panel

Click on the Auto button to adjust the hue and saturation in an image, or drag the slider to make manual adjustments. Click on the thumbnails to apply preset amounts.

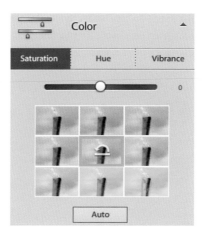

Balance panel

Drag the slider to adjust the warmth of the colors in an image and the color balance. Click on the thumbnails to apply preset amounts.

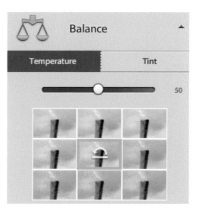

Don't forget

The Balance panel can be used to create some abstract color effects.

Sharpen panel

This can be used to apply sharpening to an image to make it clearer, either automatically with the Auto button, or the panel thumbnails, or manually with the slider.

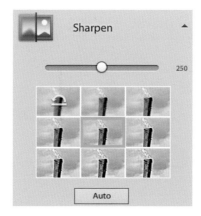

Using Guided Edit Mode

In Elements the Guided edit function has been enhanced to make it easier to perform both simple editing functions and also more complex image-editing processes that consist of a number of steps. To use the various functions of Guided edit mode:

1 Open an image and click on the **Guided** button

2 In the **Touchups** section, select a function such as Brightness and Contrast

3 Details of the selected function are displayed. Click on the **Auto Fix** button or drag the sliders to apply the effects for the selected function

4 Click on the **Done** button

Photo Effects and Photo Play

In addition to one-step Guided edits there are also more in-depth operations such as Photo Effects and Photo Play. These contain a number of editing techniques, which you are taken through in a step-by-step process to create the final effect:

1 Click on one of the options under **Photo Effects** or **Photo Play**. The Photo Effects include items such as creating depth of field effects, color effects such as high key, to give a photo a surreal brightness, and traditional photography effects such as the Lomo Camera Effect and the Orton Effect. The Photo Play effects are for special effects such as making one element appear out of the rest of the photo, a broken up Picture Stack, Pop Art effect and a Reflection of the selected image

Don't forget

For details of some of the Photo Effects and Photo Play effects, see Chapter Nine.

2 Click on each of the buttons to apply the required effects. Some of these have additional dialog boxes where settings for the effect can be applied

3 If you do not like the appearance of the photo, click on the **Reset** button to return to its original state

4 Click on the **Done** button to complete the Guided edit

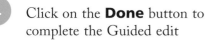

Photomerge Effects

Within Elements there are a number of Photomerge effects that can be used to combine elements from different photos to create a new image. This can be used to remove items from photos, combine elements from two, or more, photos and match the exposure from different photos.

To access the Photomerge options, select **Enhance > Photomerge** from within any of the Editor modes.

Photomerge® Group Shot...
Photomerge® Faces...
Photomerge® Scene Cleaner...
Photomerge® Panorama...
Photomerge® Exposure...
Photomerge® Style Match...

The Photomerge options are:

- **Group Shot.** This can be used to add or delete people from group shots. This is done by opening two, or more, photos of the group. Use the **Pencil** tool to merge a person from one photo into the other and the **Eraser** tool to delete any areas that you do not want copied to the new photo

Don't forget

The Pencil tool is used for several of the Photomerge options. It is used to draw over an area in a source image that is then merged into the final image.

Photomerge Group Shot

Create the perfect photo from multiple photos.

Drag a group photo to the final window. Click a different photo you wish to merge into the final photo to make it the source Image.

Pencil Tool

Eraser Tool

- **Faces.** This is an option for combining features of two faces together. This is done by opening photos of two people and then aligning the features of one so that they are merged with the other

- **Scene Cleaner.** This can be used to remove unwanted elements in a photo. This is done by using two, or more, similar photos, with elements that you want to remove, then merging the elements that you want to keep into the final photo

- **Panorama.** This can be used to create panoramas with two, or more, photos (see pages 86–88 for details)

- **Exposure.** This can be used to create a well-exposed photo from a series of photos of the same shot that have different exposures, i.e. one may be over-exposed and another under-exposed. The Photomerge effect combines the photos so that the final one is correctly exposed

- **Style Match.** This can be used to apply preset photo styles to your own photos

Beware

For the Exposure Photomerge function, all of the photos used have to be of exactly the same shot, otherwise there will be some overlap in the final image.

Panoramas

Creating panoramas

For anyone who takes landscape pictures, the desire to create a panorama occurs sooner or later. With film-based cameras, this usually involves sticking several photographs together to create the panorama, albeit a rather patchwork one. With digital images the end result can look a lot more professional and Elements has a dedicated function for achieving this: the Photomerge Panorama.

When creating a panorama there are a few rules to follow:

- If possible, use a tripod to ensure that your camera stays at the same level for all of the shots

- Keep the same exposure settings for all images

- Make sure that there is a reasonable overlap between images (about 20%). Some cameras enable you to align the correct overlap between the images

- Keep the same distance between yourself and the object you are capturing. Otherwise the end result will look out of perspective

To create a panorama:

Beware

Do not include too many images in a panorama, otherwise it could be too large for viewing or printing easily.

1. In Expert edit mode open two or more images and select **Enhance > Photomerge > Photomerge Panorama** from the Menu bar

2. Select an option for the type of panorama image that you want to create

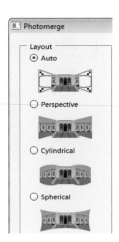

3 Click on the **Browse** button to locate images you want to use on your computer

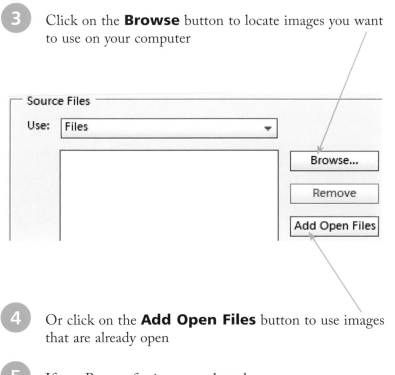

4 Or click on the **Add Open Files** button to use images that are already open

5 If you Browse for images, select them from your computer

DSCN1272   DSCN1273   DSCN1274

6 Click on the **OK** button

OK

...cont'd

7 In some instances the final image may need some additional editing. One common problem is the appearance of diagonal lines across the image, particularly in the sky region

8 Panoramas can usually be improved by applying color correction such as Brightness/Contrast and Shadows/Highlights. They can also be cropped to straighten the borders

9 An unwanted line in a panorama can be removed by cloning from a nearby area, or by selecting it and applying color correction until it is the same tone as the rest of the image. Some trial and error may be needed to achieve exactly the right look

5 Beyond the Basics

Since Elements is based on the full version of Photoshop, it contains a number of powerful features for image editing. This chapter looks at some of these features and how to use them.

Hue and Saturation

The hue and saturation command can be used to edit the color elements of an image. However, it works slightly differently from other commands, such as those for the brightness and contrast. There are three areas that are covered by the hue and saturation command: color, color strength and lightness. To adjust the hue and saturation of an image:

1 Open an image

2 Select **Enhance > Adjust Color > Adjust Hue/ Saturation** from the Menu bar, in either Expert or Quick edit modes

90

3 Drag this slider to adjust the hue of the image, i.e. change the colors in the image

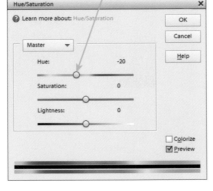

4 Drag this slider to adjust the saturation, i.e. the intensity of colors in the image

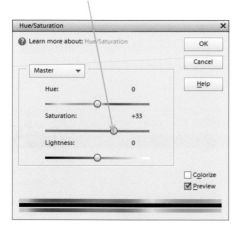

Don't forget

The Lightness option is similar to adjusting image brightness.

5 Check on the **Colorize** box to color the image with the hue of the currently-selected foreground color in the Color Picker, which is located at the bottom of the Toolbox

Hot tip

The Colorize option can be used to create some interesting "color wash" effects. Try altering the Hue slider once the Colorize box has been checked on.

Don't forget

For more on working with color and the Color Picker, see Chapter Eight.

6 Click on the **OK** button to apply any changes that have been made

OK

91

Histogram

The histogram is a device that displays the tonal range of the pixels in an image, and it can be used for very precise editing of an image. The histogram (**Window > Histogram** in Expert edit mode) is a graph which displays how the pixels in an image are distributed across the image, from the darkest (black) to the lightest (white) points. Another way of considering the histogram is that it displays the values of an image's highlights, midtones and shadows:

Highlights

Midtones

Shadows

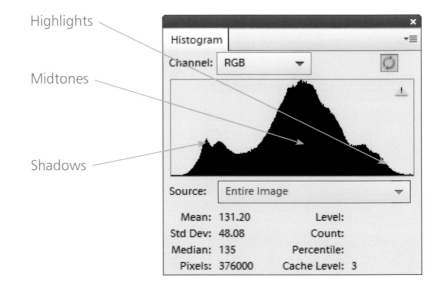

Highlights

Midtones

Shadows

Ideally, the histogram should show a reasonably consistent range of tonal distribution, indicating an image that has good contrast and detail:

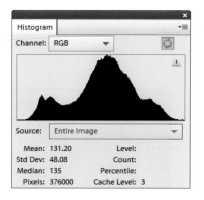

However, if the tonal range is bunched at one end of the graph, this indicates that the image is under-exposed or over-exposed:

Over-exposure

Under-exposure

Hot tip

If the histogram is left open, it will update automatically as editing changes are made to an image. This gives a good idea of how effective the changes are.

93

Levels

While the histogram displays the tonal range of an image, the Levels function can be used to edit this range. Any changes made using the Levels function will then be visible in the histogram. Levels allow you to redistribute pixels between the darkest and lightest points in an image, and also to set these points manually if you want to. To use the Levels function:

Hot tip

The Levels function can be used to adjust the tonal range of a specific area of an image, by first making a selection and then using the Levels dialog box. For more details on selecting areas see Chapter Six.

1 Open an image

94

Don't forget

In the Levels dialog box, the graph is the same as the one shown in the histogram.

2 Select **Enhance > Adjust Lighting > Levels** from the Menu bar, in either Expert or Quick edit modes

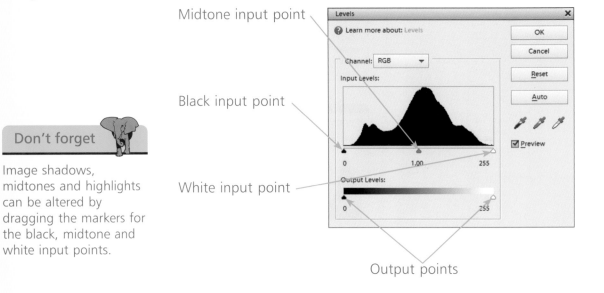

Midtone input point

Black input point

White input point

Output points

Don't forget

Image shadows, midtones and highlights can be altered by dragging the markers for the black, midtone and white input points.

③ Drag the black point and the white point sliders to, or beyond, the first pixels denoted in the graph to increase the contrast

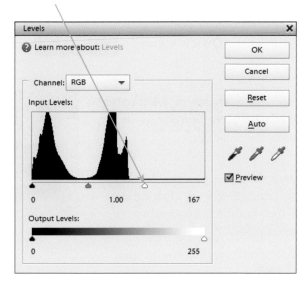

④ Drag the output sliders towards the middle to decrease the contrast

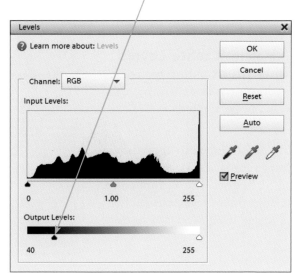

Quick and Guided Levels

Levels can also be applied within the Quick and Guided edit modes in the Editor. To do this:

Quick Levels

1 Click on the **Quick** button

2 Click on the **Levels** panel and select the **Shadows**, **Midtones** or **Highlights** buttons to set the levels for these areas

3 Drag the slider to apply levels to the selected area, or click on one of the thumbnails to apply a preset value

Guided Levels

1 Click on the **Guided** button

2 Click on the **Levels** button

3 Click on the **Create Levels Adjustment** button to create an adjustment layer, to which the levels can be applied

4 Drag these sliders to apply levels settings for shadows, midtones and highlights. This is applied to the adjustment level, rather than the image itself

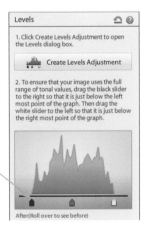

5 Click on the **Done** button

Unsharp Mask

Although sharpening is a useful technique for improving the overall definition of an image, it can sometimes appear too harsh and "jaggy". For a more subtle effect, the Unsharp Mask can be used. This works by increasing the contrast between light and dark pixels in an image. To use the Unsharp Mask:

1 Open an image in Expert edit mode or Quick edit mode that you want to sharpen

2 Select the **Enhance > Unsharp Mask** option from the Menu bar

3 Apply the appropriate settings in the **Unsharp Mask** dialog box and click on the **OK** button

4 The contrast between light and dark pixels is increased, giving the impression of a clearer, or sharper, image

Don't forget

The settings for the Unsharp Mask are: Amount, which determines the amount to increase the contrast between pixels; Radius, which determines how many pixels will have the sharpening applied to them in an affected area; and Threshold, which determines how different a pixel has to be from its neighbor before sharpening is applied.

Don't forget

Quick edit and Guided edit modes also have an automated Sharpen feature that is available from a button in the panels bin.

Importing RAW Images

RAW images are those in which the digital data has not been processed in any way, or converted into any specific file format, by the camera when they were captured. These produce high quality images and are usually available on higher specification digital cameras. However, RAW is becoming more common in consumer digital cameras and they can be downloaded in Elements in the same way as any other image. Once the RAW images are accessed, the Camera Raw dialog box opens so that a variety of editing functions can be applied to the image. RAW images act as a digital negative and have to be saved into another format before they can be used in the conventional way. To edit RAW images:

Beware

RAW images are much larger in file size than the same versions captured as JPEGs.

Don't forget

The RAW format should be used if you want to make manual changes to an image to achieve the highest possible quality.

1 Open a RAW image in the Editor or from the Organizer

2 In the Camera RAW dialog box, editing functions that are usually performed when an image is captured can be made manually

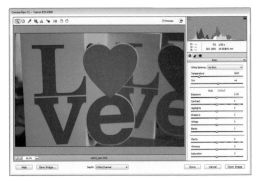

3 Click here to adjust the White Balance in the image

White Balance: As Shot

As Shot
Auto
Daylight
Cloudy
Shade
Tungsten
Fluorescent
Flash
Custom

4 Drag these sliders to adjust the Color Temperature and Tint in the image

Temperature   3600

Tint   +6

...cont'd

5 Drag these sliders to adjust the Exposure, Shadows, Brightness, Contrast and Saturation in the image

Auto   Default

Exposure	0.00
Contrast	0
Highlights	0
Shadows	0
Whites	0
Blacks	0

6 Click on the **Detail** tab and drag these sliders to adjust the Sharpness and Noise in the image

Detail

Sharpening

Amount	25
Radius	1.0
Detail	25
Masking	0

Noise Reduction

Luminance	0
Luminance Detail	
Luminance Contrast	
Color	25
Color Detail	50

7 Click on the **Open Image** button. This opens the image in Expert edit mode, from where it can also be saved as a standard file format, such as JPEG

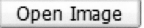

Open Image

66

Image Size

The physical size of a digital image can sometimes be a confusing issue, as it is frequently dealt with under the term "resolution". Unfortunately, resolution can be applied to a number of areas of digital imaging: image resolution, monitor resolution, print size and print resolution.

Image resolution

The resolution of an image is determined by the number of pixels in it. This is counted as a vertical and a horizontal value, e.g. 4000 x 3000. When multiplied together it gives the overall resolution, i.e. 12,000,000 pixels in this case. This is frequently the headline figure quoted by the manufacturers, e.g. 12 million pixels (or 12 megapixels). To view the image resolution in Elements:

Hot tip

To view an image on a monitor at its actual size, or the size at which it will currently be printed, select the **Zoom** tool from the Toolbox and select **1:1** or **Print Size** from the Tool Options panel.

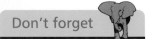

Don't forget

The Resolution figure under the Document Size heading is used to determine the size at which the image will be printed. If this is set to 72 pixels/inch, then the onscreen size and the printed size should be roughly the same.

1 Select **Image > Resize > Image Size** from the Menu bar

2 The image size is displayed here (in pixels)

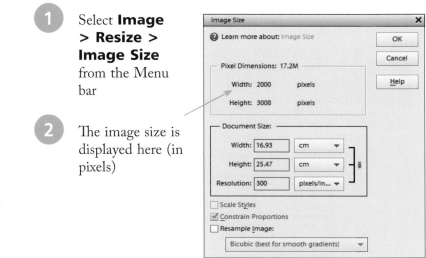

Monitor resolution

Most modern computer monitors display digital images at between 72 and 96 pixels per inch (PPI). This means that every inch of the screen contains approximately this number of pixels. So, for an image being displayed at 100%, the onscreen size will be the number of pixels horizontally divided by 72 (or 96 depending on the monitor) and the same vertically. In the above example, this would mean the image would be viewed at 34 inches by 45 inches approximately (2448/72 and 3264/72) on a monitor. In modern web browsers this is usually adjusted so that the whole image is accommodated on the viewable screen.

Document size (print resolution)

Pixels in an image are not a set size, which means that images can be printed in a variety of sizes, simply by contracting or expanding the available pixels. This is done by changing the resolution in the Document Size section of the Image Size dialog box. (When dealing with document size, think of this as the size of the printed document.) To set the size at which an image will be printed:

Hot tip

The higher the print resolution, the better the final printed image. Aim for a minimum of 200 pixels per inch for the best printed output.

 Select **Image > Resize > Image Size** from the Menu bar

Hot tip

To work out the size at which an image will be printed, divide the pixel dimensions (height and width) by the resolution value under the Document Size heading.

2 Change the resolution here (or change the Width and Height of the document size). Make sure the Resample Image box is not checked

Image Size	✕
❷ Learn more about: Image Size	OK
	Cancel
Pixel Dimensions: 17.2M	Help
Width: 2000 pixels	
Height: 3008 pixels	
Document Size:	
Width: 33.87 cm ▼	
Height: 50.94 cm ▼	
Resolution: 150 pixels/in... ▼	
☐ Scale Styles	
☑ Constrain Proportions	
☐ Resample Image:	
Bicubic (best for smooth gradients) ▼	

Don't forget

The print resolution determines how many pixels are used in each inch of the printed image (PPI). However, the number of colored dots used to represent each pixel on the paper is determined by the printer resolution, measured in dots per inch (DPI). So if the print resolution is 72 PPI and the printer resolution is 2880 DPI, each pixel will be represented by 40 colored dots, i.e. 2880 divided by 72.

3 By changing one value, the other two are updated too. Click on the **OK** button

― Document Size: ――――

Width:	20	cm ▼
Height:	30.08	cm ▼
Resolution:	254	pixels/in... ▼

OK

Resampling Images

All digital images can be increased or decreased in size. This involves adding or removing pixels from the image. Decreasing the size of an image is relatively straightforward and involves removing redundant pixels. However, increasing the size of an image involves adding pixels by digital guesswork. To do this, Elements looks at the existing pixels and works out the nearest match for the ones that are to be added. Increasing or decreasing the size of a digital image is known as "resampling".

Resampling

Resampling down decreases the size of the image and it is more effective than resampling up. To do this:

Don't forget

The process of adding pixels to an image to increase its size is known as "interpolation".

Beware

Since it involves digital guesswork by Elements, resampling up results in inferior image quality.

Hot tip

To keep the same resolution for an image, resample it by changing the Pixel Dimensions' height and width. To keep the same Document Size (i.e. the size at which it will be printed) resample it by changing the resolution.

Beware

Make sure the Constrain Proportions box is checked on if you want the image to be increased or decreased in size proportionally, rather than just one value being altered independently of the other.

1 Select **Image > Resize > Image Size** from the Menu bar

2 Check on the **Resample Image** box

3 Resample the image by changing the pixel dimensions, the height and width or the resolution

Pixel Dimensions: 17.2M (was 17.2M)

Width: 1999 pixels

Height: 3007 pixels

Document Size:

Width: 16.93 cm

Height: 25.46 cm

Resolution: 300 pixels/in...

☐ Scale Styles
☑ Constrain Proportions
☑ Resample Image:

4 Changing any of the values above alters the physical size of the image. Click on the **OK** button

Pixel Dimensions: 4.30M (was 17.2M)

Width: 1000 pixels

Height: 1504 pixels

6 Selecting Areas

The true power of digital image editing comes into its own when you are able to select areas of an image and edit them independently. This chapter looks at the various ways that selections can be made and edited within Elements.

About Selections

One of the most important aspects of image editing is the ability to select areas within an image. This can be used in a number of different ways:

- Selecting an object to apply an editing technique to it (such as changing the brightness or contrast) without affecting the rest of the image

- Selecting a particular color in an image

- Selecting an area on which to apply a special effect

- Selecting an area to remove

Expert edit mode has several tools that can be used to select items, and there are also a number of editing functions that can be applied to selections.

Two examples of how selections can be used are:

Don't forget

Once a selection has been made it stays selected, even when another tool is activated, to allow for editing to take place.

1. Select an area within an image and delete it

Hot tip

The best way to deselect a selection is to click on it once with one of the selection tools, preferably the one used to make the selection.

2. Select an area and add a color or special effect

Marquee Tools

There are two options for the Marquee tool: the Rectangular Marquee tool and the Elliptical Marquee tool. Both of these can be used to make symmetrical selections. To use the Marquee tools:

1 Select either the **Rectangular** or the **Elliptical Marquee** tool from the Toolbox. Select the required options from the Tool Options panel

2 Make a symmetrical selection with one of the tools by clicking and dragging on an image

Elliptical selection   Rectangular selection

Hot tip

To make a selection that is exactly square or round, hold down Shift when dragging with the Rectangular Marquee tool or the Elliptical Marquee tool respectively.

Lasso Tools

There are three options for the Lasso tools, which can be used to make freehand selections. To use these:

Lasso tool

1 Select the **Lasso** tool from the Toolbox and select the required options from the Tool Options panel

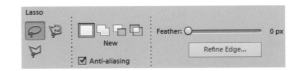

2 Make a freehand selection by clicking and dragging around an object

Polygonal Lasso tool

1 Select the **Polygonal Lasso** tool from the Toolbox and select the required options from the Tool Options panel

2 Make a selection by clicking on specific points around an object, and then dragging to the next point

Magnetic Lasso tool

1 Select the **Magnetic Lasso** tool from the Toolbox and select the required options from the Tool Options panel

2 Click once on an image to create the first anchor point

3 Make a selection by dragging continuously around an object. The selection line snaps to the closest strongest edge, i.e. the one with the most contrast. Fastening points are added as the selection is made

Don't forget

In the Tool Options panel for the Magnetic Lasso tool, the Contrast value determines the amount of contrast there has to be between colors for the selection line to snap to them. A high value detects lines with a high contrast and vice versa.

Don't forget

The Frequency setting in the Tool Options panel determines how quickly the fastening points are inserted as a selection is being made. A high value places the fastening points more quickly than a low value.

Magic Wand Tool

The Magic Wand tool can be used to select areas of the same, or similar, color. To do this:

108

1 Select the **Magic Wand** tool from the Toolbox and select the required options from the Tool Options panel

2 Click on a color to select all of the adjacent pixels that are the same, or similar, color, depending on the options selected from the Tool Options panel

Selection Brush Tool

The Selection Brush tool can be used to select areas by using a brush-like stroke. Unlike with the Marquee or Lasso tools, the area selected by the Selection Brush tool is the one directly below where the tool moves. To make a selection with the Selection Brush tool (this is also available in Quick edit mode):

 Select the **Selection Brush** tool from the Toolbox and select the required options from the Tool Options panel

Don't forget

The Selection Brush tool can be used to select an area, or to mask an area. This can be determined in the Selection box in the Tool Options panel.

2 Click and drag to make a selection

3 The selection area is underneath the borders of the Selection Brush tool

Quick Selection Tool

The Quick Selection tool can be used to select areas of similar color by drawing over the general area, without having to make a specific selection. To do this:

 Select the **Quick Selection** tool from the Toolbox

 Select the required options from the Tool Options panel

Don't forget

The Quick Selection tool is also available from the Quick edit mode Toolbox.

110

 Draw over an area, or part of an area, to select all of the similarly-colored pixels

Smart Brush Tool

The Smart Brush tool can be used to quickly select large areas in an image (in a similar way to the Quick Selection tool) and then have effects applied automatically to the selected area. To do this:

1 Open the image to which you want to apply changes

Don't forget

Multiple editing effects can be applied with the Smart Brush tool within the same image. This usually requires selecting different parts of the image and selecting the required effect.

2 Select the **Smart Brush** tool from the Toolbox

3 Select the editing effect you want to apply to the area selected by the Smart Brush tool, from the Tool Options panel

4 Select **Brush size** for the Smart Brush tool, from the Tool Options panel

5 Drag the Smart Brush tool over an area of the image. In the left-hand image below, the building has been selected and brightened; in the right-hand image the sky has been selected and enhanced

Inverting a Selection

This can be a useful option if you have edited a selection and then want to edit the rest of the image without affecting the area you have just selected. To do this:

1 Make a selection

2 Choose **Select > Inverse** from the Menu bar

3 The selection becomes inverted, i.e. if a background object was selected the foreground is now selected

Feathering

Feathering is a technique that can be used to soften the edges of a selection by making them slightly blurry. This can be used if you are pasting a selection into another image, or if you want to soften the edges around a portrait of an individual. To do this:

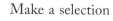 Make a selection

2 Choose **Select > Feather** from the Menu bar

3 Enter a Feather value (the number of pixels around the radius of the selection that will be blurred). Click on the **OK** button

Feather Selection

Learn more about: Feather Selection

OK

Cancel

Feather Radius: 5 pixels

4 Invert the selection, as shown on the previous page, and delete the background by pressing **Delete** on the keyboard. This will leave the selection around the subject with softened edges

Don't forget

Feathering can also be selected from the Tool Options panel once a Marquee tool is selected, and before the selection has been made.

Hot tip

If required, crop the final image so that the feathered subject is more prominent.

Editing Selections

When you have made a selection, you can edit it in a number of ways:

Moving a selection
Make a selection and select the **Move** tool from the Toolbox. Drag the selection to move it to a new location.

Changing the selection area
Make a selection with a selection tool. With the same tool selected, click and drag within the selection area to move it over another part of the image.

Adding to a selection
Make a selection and click on this button in the Tool Options panel Make another selection to create a single larger selection. The two selections do not have to intersect.

Intersecting with a selection
To create a selection by intersecting two existing selections: make a selection and click on this button in the Tool Options panel. Make another selection that intersects the first. The intersected area will become the selection.

Expanding a selection
To expand a selection by a specific number of pixels: make a selection and choose **Select > Modify > Expand** from the Menu bar. In the **Expand Selection** dialog box, enter the amount by which you want the selection expanded.

Growing a selection
The Grow command can be used on a selection when it has been made with the Magic Wand tool, and some of the pixels within the selection have been omitted. To do this:

Make a selection with the **Magic Wand** tool and make the required choices from the Tool Options panel. Choose **Select > Grow** from the Menu bar. Depending on the choices in the Tool Options panel, the omitted pixels will be included in the selection.

Beware

Once an area has been moved and deselected, it cannot then be selected independently again, unless it has been copied and pasted onto a separate layer.

Don't forget

To deselect a selection, click once inside the selection area with the tool that was used to make the selection.

7 Layers

Layers provide the means to add numerous elements to an image, and edit them independently from one another. This chapter looks at how to use layers to expand your creative possibilities.

Layering Images

Layering is a technique that enables you to add additional elements to an image, and place them on separate layers, so that they can be edited and manipulated independently from other elements in the image. It is like creating an image using transparent sheets of film: each layer is independent of the others but, when they are combined, a composite image is created. This is an extremely versatile technique for working with digital images.

By using layers, several different elements can be combined to create a composite image:

Original image

Final image
With text and a shape added (two additional layers have been added).

Layers Panel

The use of layers within Elements is done within Expert edit mode and is governed by the Layers panel. When an image is first opened it is shown in the Layers panel as the Background layer. While this remains as the Background layer it cannot be moved above any other layers. However, it can be converted into a normal layer, in which case it operates in the same way as any other layer. To convert a Background layer into a normal one:

1. Click on the **Layers** button on the Taskbar

2. The open image is shown in the Layers panel as the Background

3. Double-click on the layer. Enter a name for it and click on the **OK** button

4. The Background layer is converted into a normal layer in the Layers panel

Hot tip

The Background layer can also be converted into a normal one by applying the Background Eraser tool and the Magic Eraser tool.

117

Don't forget

The Layers panel menu can be accessed from the button in the top right-hand corner of the Layers panel.

Adding Layers

New blank layers can be added whenever you want to include new content within an image. This could be part of another image that has been copied and pasted, a whole new image, text or an object. To add a new layer:

1 Click here on the Layers panel

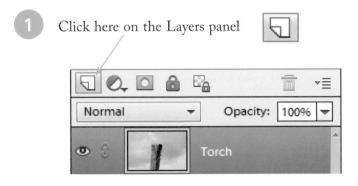

2 Double-click on the layer name and overtype to give the layer a new name

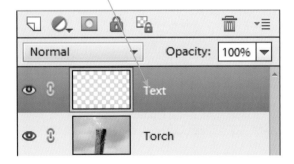

3 With the new layer selected in the Layers panel, add content to the layer. This will be visible over the layer, or layers, below it

Fill and Adjustment Layers

Fill and adjustment layers can be added to images to give an effect behind or above the main subject. To do this:

1 Open the Layers panel and select a layer. The fill or adjustment layer will be placed directly above the selected layer

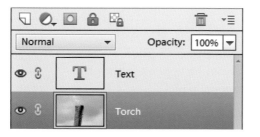

2 Click here at the bottom of the Layers panel

3 Select one of the fill or adjustment options. The fill options are **Solid Color, Gradient** or **Pattern Fill**

Solid Color...
Gradient...
Pattern...

Levels...
Brightness/Contrast...

Hue/Saturation...
Gradient Map...
Photo Filter...

Invert
Threshold...
Posterize...

Don't forget

The Adjustments panel is used for Levels, Brightness/Contrast, Hue/Saturation, Gradient Map, Photo Filter, Threshold and Posterize.

...cont'd

4 For a Solid Color, Gradient or Pattern Fill, the required fill is selected from a dialog box and this is added to the selected layer

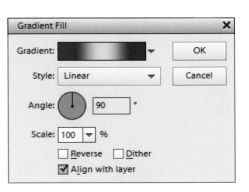

5 For an adjustment option, settings can be applied within the Adjustments panel

6 Once fill and adjustment settings have been applied, the effect can be edited by changing the opacity. This is done by dragging this slider

7 The opacity level determines how much of the image is visible through the fill or adjustment layer

Working with Layers

Moving layers

The order in which layers are arranged in the Layers panel is known as the stacking order. It is possible to change a layer's position in the stacking order, which affects how it is viewed in the composite image. To do this:

 Click and drag a layer within the Layers panel to change its stacking order

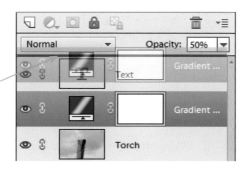

Beware

Layers can be deleted by selecting them and clicking on the Trashcan icon in the Layers panel. However, this also deletes all of the content on that layer.

Hiding layers

Layers can be hidden while you are working on other parts of an image. However, the layer is still part of the composite image – it has not been removed. To hide a layer:

1 Click here so that a line appears through the eye icon. Click again to remove the line and reveal the layer

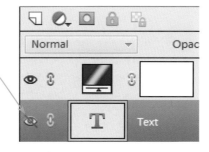

Locking layers

Layers can be locked, so that they cannot be edited accidentally while you are working on other parts of an image. To do this:

1 Select a layer and click here so that the padlock is activated. The padlock also appears on the layer

Layer Masks

Because layers can be separated within an individual image there is a certain amount of versatility, in terms of how different layers can interact with each other. One of these ways is to create a layer mask. This is a top-level layer, through which an area is removed so that the layer below is revealed. To do this:

1 Open an image. It will be displayed as the Background in the Layers panel. Double-click on this to select it

122

2 Give the layer a new name and click on the **OK** button

New Layer ✕

Name: Tree   OK

☐ Use Previous Layer to Create Clipping Mask   Cancel

Mode: Normal ▾   Opacity: 100 ▾ %

3 Click on the **Graphics** button on the Taskbar to access the Graphics panel

Graphics

4 Select a background and double-click on it to add it to the current image. Initially, this is added below the open image. Rename the new layer

below the open image. Rename the new layer

5 Drag the added layer above the original image (this can also be done by selecting an area in

another image, copying it and then pasting it above the existing image)

6 The background image now covers the original one

Beware

Make sure that all layers are converted into normal layers, rather than background ones.

...cont'd

7 Click here to apply a layer mask to the top layer

8 Select either one of the **Marquee** tools, the **Lasso** tools, or the **Brush** tool from the Toolbox

Don't forget

If the Brush tool is used to create the layer mask, this is done by drawing over the top layer of the image. As this is done, the layer below will be revealed. Change the level of Opacity in the Tool Options panel to change the amount of the layer below that is shown through the top layer of the image.

9 Select an area on the top layer and delete it to display the image below it (**Edit > Delete** from the Menu bar)

10 In the Layers panel, the area that has been removed is displayed here

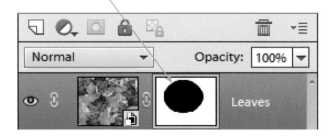

Opacity

The opacity of a layer can be set to determine how much of the layer below is visible through the selected layer. To do this:

1 Select a layer either in the Layers panel or by clicking on the relevant item within an image

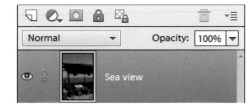

2 Click here and drag the slider to achieve the required level of opacity. The greater the amount of opacity, the less transparent the selected layer becomes

3 The opacity setting determines how much of the background, or the layer below, is visible through the selected one and this can be used to create some interesting artistic effects, including a watermark effect if the opacity is applied to a single layer with nothing behind it

Hot tip

The background behind an image, to which opacity has been applied, can be changed within the Preferences section by selecting **Edit > Preferences** from the Menu bar and then selecting Transparency and editing the Grid Colors box.

Saving Layers

Once an image has been created using two or more layers, there are two ways in which the composite image can be saved: in a proprietary Photoshop format, in which case individual layers are maintained, or in a general file format, where all of the layers will be merged into a single one. The advantage of the former is that individual elements can still be edited within the image, independently of other items. In general, it is good practice to save layered images in both a Photoshop and a non-Photoshop format. To save layered images in a Photoshop format:

1 Select **File > Save As** from the Menu bar

2 Make sure Photoshop (*.PSD, *.PDD) is selected as the format

3 Make sure the Layers box is checked on

4 Click on the **Save** button

To save in a non-Photoshop format, select **File > Save As** from the Menu bar. Select the file format from the Format box (such as JPEG or TIFF) and click on the **Save** button. The Layers box will not be available.

8 Text and Drawing Tools

Elements offers a lot more than just the ability to edit digital images. It also has options for adding and formatting text and creating a variety of graphical objects. This chapter looks at how to add text and also include drawing objects.

Adding and Formatting Text

Text can be added to images in Elements and this can be used to create a wide range of items, such as cards, brochures and posters. To add text to an image:

Beware

Use the Vertical Type tool sparingly, as this is not a natural way for the eye to read text. Use it with small amounts of text, for effect.

Don't forget

Anti-aliasing is a technique that smooths out the jagged edges that can sometimes appear with text when viewed on a computer monitor. Anti-aliasing is created by adding pixels to the edges of text, so that it blends more smoothly with the background.

 Select the **Horizontal** or **Vertical Type** tool from the Toolbox

 Drag on the image with the Type tool to create a text box

3 Make the required formatting selections from the Tool Options panel

Type tools   Font type   Font size

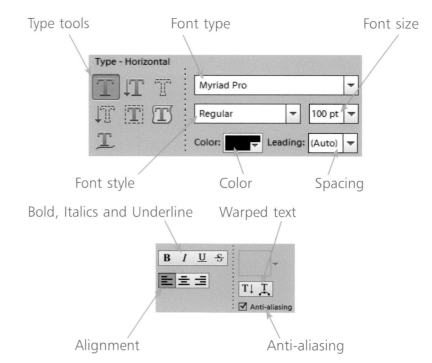

Font style   Color   Spacing

Bold, Italics and Underline   Warped text

Alignment   Anti-aliasing

4 Type the text onto the image. This is automatically placed on a new layer at the top of the stacking order in the Layers panel

5 To move the text, select it with the **Move** tool, click and drag it to a new position

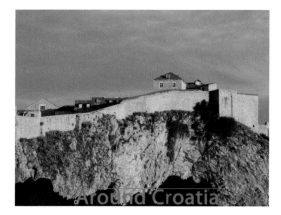

To format text that has already been entered:

1 Select a **Type** tool and drag it over a piece of text to select it

2 Make the changes in the Tool Options panel, as shown in Step 3 on the facing page

3 Click on the green tick to accept the text entry

Customizing Text

As well as adding standard text, it is also possible to add text to follow a selection, a shape or a custom path. This can be done within Expert edit and Quick edit modes.

Adding text to a selection
To add text to a selection within an image:

1 Click on the **Type** tool and select the **Text on Selection** tool option

2 Drag over an area of an image to make a selection

Don't forget

In Expert edit mode, select the Move tool and click and drag the text to move it and also the selection area.

3 Click on the green tick to accept the selection

4 Click anywhere on the selection and add text. By default, this will be displayed along the outside of the selection

5 Format the text in the same way as with standard text

Adding text to a shape

To add text to a shape within an image:

 1 Click on the **Type** tool and select the **Text on Shape** tool option

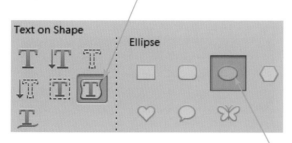

2 Click here in the Tool Options panel to select a shape

3 Drag over an area of an image to create a shape

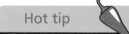

Hot tip

Once customized text has been added and accepted it can still be edited in the same way as standard text, by using the Horizontal Type Tool and selecting the customized text.

4 Click anywhere on the shape and add text. Click on the green tick as in Step 3 on the previous page

5 Format the text in the same way as with standard text

...cont'd

Adding text to a custom path

Text can also be added to a custom path that you draw on an image. To do this:

 1 Open the image onto which you want to create text on a custom path

 2 Click on the **Type** tool and select the **Text on Custom Path** tool option. Make sure the **Draw** button is also selected

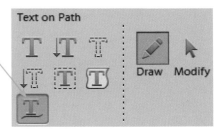

3 Draw a custom path on the image

4 Click on the green tick to accept the text path

5 Click anywhere on the custom path and add text

6 Format the text in the same way as with standard text

7 Click on the **Modify** tool in the Tool Options panel. This activates the markers along the custom path

8 Drag the markers to move the position of the custom path

9 The custom path can be used to position text in a variety of ways around objects or people

Beware

If there is too much text on a custom path it can become jumbled, particularly if you adjust the markers on the path.

Distorting Text

In addition to producing standard text, it is also possible to create some dramatic effects by distorting text. To do this:

134

1 Enter plain text and select it by dragging a **Type** tool over it

2 Click the **Create Warped Text** button on the Tool Options panel

3 Click here and select one of the options in the Warp Text dialog box. Click on the **OK** button

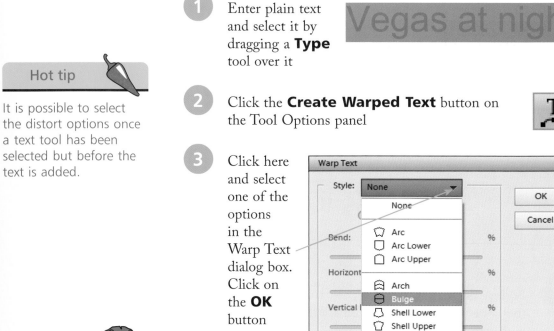

4 The selected effect is applied to the text

Hot tip

It is possible to select the distort options once a text tool has been selected but before the text is added.

Beware

Use text distortion sparingly, as it can become annoying if it is overdone.

Text and Shape Masks

Text Masks can be used to reveal an area of an image showing through the text. This can be used to produce eye-catching headings and slogans. To do this:

1 Select the **Horizontal** or **Vertical Type Mask** tool from the Toolbox

2 Click on an image, then enter and format text as you would for normal text. A red mask is applied to the image when the mask text is entered

Hot tip

Text Mask effects work best if the text used is fairly large in size. In some cases it is a good idea to use bold text, as this is wider than standard text.

135

3 Press **Enter** or click the **Move** tool to border the mask text with dots

...cont'd

 Select **Edit > Copy** from the Menu bar

Select **File > New** from the Menu bar and create a new file

Select **Edit > Paste** from the Menu bar to paste the text mask into the new file

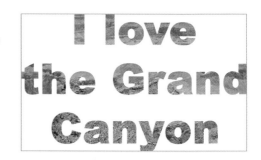

Cookie Cutter masks

A similar effect can be created with shape masks by using the Cookie Cutter tool:

Select the **Cookie Cutter** tool in the Toolbox and click here to select a particular style in the Tool Options panel

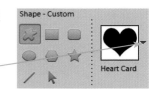

Drag on an image to create a cut-out effect

Adding Shapes

Another way to add extra style to your images is through the use of shapes. There are several types of symmetrical shapes that can be added to images, and also a range of custom ones. To add shapes to an image:

1 Click on the **Custom Shape** tool and select the type of shape you want to create

2 Select a color here

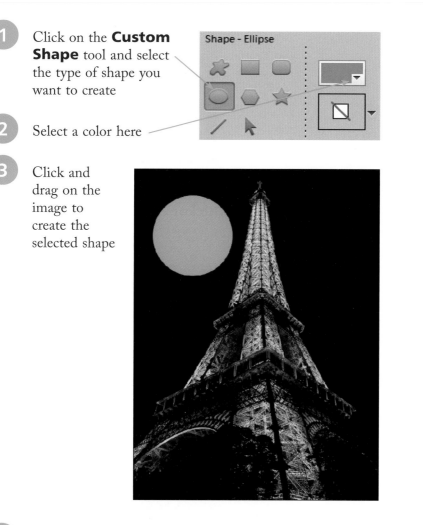

3 Click and drag on the image to create the selected shape

4 If you want to change the color of a shape, click here in the Tool Options panel and select a new color. This can either be done before the shape is created or it can be used to edit the color of an existing shape, when selected with the **Move** tool

Paint Bucket Tool

The Paint Bucket tool can be used to add a solid color to a selection or an area in an image. To do this:

138

1 Open the image to which you want to apply the Paint Bucket

2 Select the **Paint Bucket** tool from the Toolbox

3 Select the **Opacity** and **Tolerance** in the Tool Options panel. The Tolerance determines how much of an image is affected by the Paint Bucket

4 Click once on an area of solid color with the Paint Bucket tool. The color in Step 2 will be applied

Gradient Tool

The Gradient tool can be used to add a gradient fill to a selection or an entire image. To do this:

1 Select an area in an image or select an object

139

2 Select the **Gradient** tool from the Toolbox

3 Click here in the Tool Options panel to select pre-set gradient fills

4 Click on a gradient style to apply it as the default

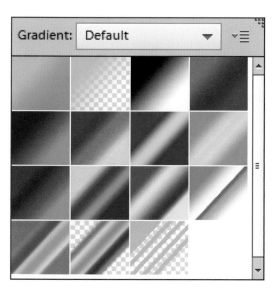

Beware

If no selection is made for a gradient fill, the effect will be applied to the entire selected layer.

Hot tip

The default gradient effect in the Tool Options panel is created with the currently-selected foreground and background colors within the Toolbox.

...cont'd

5 Click here in the Tool Options panel to access the **Gradient Editor** dialog box

Gradient

Edit...

6 Click and drag the sliders to change the amount of a particular color in the gradient

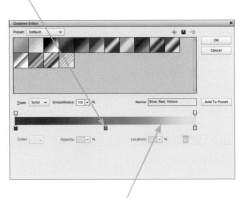

7 Click along here to add a new color marker. Click on the **OK** button

8 Click an icon in the Tool Options bar to select a gradient style

Radial

9 Click and drag within the original selection to specify the start and end points of the gradient effect

Brush and Pencil Tools

The Brush and Pencil tools work in a similar way and can be used to create lines of varying thickness and style. To do this:

1 Select the **Brush** tool or the **Pencil** tool from the Toolbox

2 Select the required options from the Tool Options panel

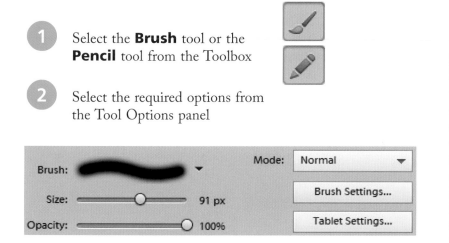

3 Click and drag to create lines on an image. (The lines are placed directly on the image. To add lines without altering the background image, add a new layer above the background and add the lines on this layer. They will then be visible over the background.)

Impressionist Brush Tool

The Impressionist Brush tool can be used to create a dappled effect over an image, similar to that of an impressionist painting. To do this:

 Select the **Impressionist Brush** tool from the Toolbox

 Select the required options from the Tool Options panel

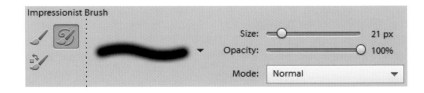

3 Click and drag over an image to create an impressionist effect

If the brush size is too large for the Impressionist Brush tool, it can result in the effect being too extreme and a lot of definition being lost in an image.

Working with Color

All of the text and drawing tools make extensive use of color. Elements provides a number of methods for selecting colors, and also for working with them.

Foreground and background colors

At the bottom of the Toolbox there are two colored squares. These represent the currently-selected foreground and background colors. The foreground color, which is the most frequently used, is the one that is applied to drawing objects, such as fills and lines, and also text. The background color is used for items, such as gradient fills, and for areas that have been removed with the Eraser tool.

Foreground color   Swap foreground and background colors

Set foreground to black   Background color
and background to white

Hot tip

Whenever the foreground or background color squares are clicked on, the Eyedropper tool is automatically activated. This can be used to select a color from anywhere on your screen, instead of using the Color Picker.

143

Color Picker

The Color Picker can be used to select a new color for the foreground or background color. To do this:

1   Click once on the foreground or the background color square, as required

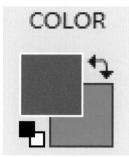

...cont'd

2 In the Color Picker, click to select a color

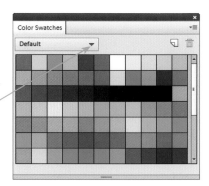

Hot tip

If you are going to be using images on the Web, check on the **Only Web Colors** box. This will display a different range of colors, which are known as web-safe colors. This means that they will appear the same on any type of web browser.

3 Click on the **OK** button

OK

Don't forget

When the cursor is moved over a color in the Color Swatches panel, the tooltip displays a description of the color, e.g. RGB Green, or Pastel Red.

Color Swatches panel

The Color Swatches panel can be used to access different color panels that can then be used to select the foreground and background colors. To do this:

1 Select **Window > Color Swatches** from the Menu bar

2 Click here to access the available panels

9 Artistic Effects

*Adding special effects is
one of the fun things about
digital images. This chapter
shows how to add artwork
and create stunning effects
for your photos to give them
the "wow" factor to stun
family and friends.*

About Graphics and Effects

Applying artistic effects can be one of the most satisfying parts of digital image editing: it is quick and the results can be dramatic. Elements has a range of Graphics and Effects that can be applied to images. To use these:

1 In Expert edit mode, click on the **Graphics** button

2 Within the Graphics panel click here to select a category for a particular topic

3 Click here to see all of the options for a particular category. Double-click on an item in the Graphics panel to add it to the currently-active image

Accessing Effects

To apply special effects to an open image in the Editor:

 1 In Expert edit mode, click on the **Effects** button

Effects

 Don't forget

In Quick and Guided edit modes, the filters can be accessed from the **Filter** menu on the Menu bar.

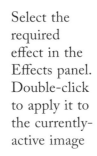 **2** Select the required effect in the Effects panel. Double-click to apply it to the currently-active image

 3 Some effects, such as Filters, have additional dialog boxes (see page 148) in which a variety of settings can be specified in relation to how the effect operates and appears. For others, the effect is applied immediately

 Hot tip

Many of the items in the Effects panel can be applied by double-clicking on them, or dragging them onto the image.

147

Adding Filters

As shown on the previous page, filters can be accessed from the Effects panel in Expert edit mode. They can also be accessed and applied from the Menu bar in any of the Editor modes. To add and modify filters:

 1 In any of the Editor modes, open the photo to which you want to apply a filter effect

2 Select **Filter** from the Menu bar and select one of the filter categories and sub-categories

3 Some filter effects have a dialog box where additional settings can be applied

4 Click on one of the Presets options to apply this automatically to the photo

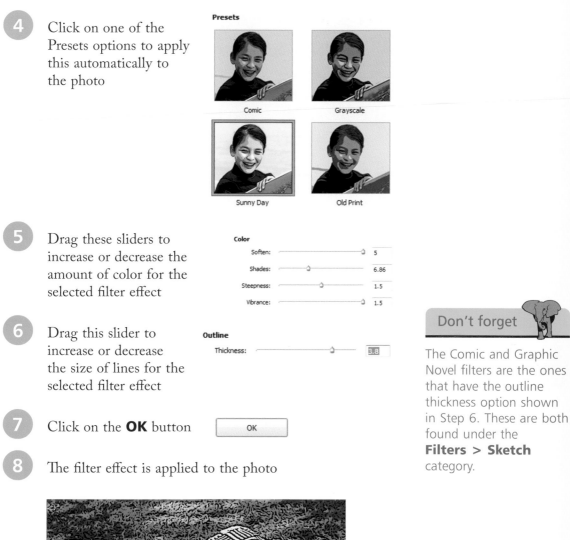

Presets

Comic   Grayscale

Sunny Day   Old Print

5 Drag these sliders to increase or decrease the amount of color for the selected filter effect

Color

Soften: ———————————○ 5

Shades: ———○———————— 6.86

Steepness: ————○——————— 1.5

Vibrance: ———————————○ 1.5

6 Drag this slider to increase or decrease the size of lines for the selected filter effect

Outline

Thickness: —————————○—— 3.8

7 Click on the **OK** button

OK

8 The filter effect is applied to the photo

Don't forget

The Comic and Graphic Novel filters are the ones that have the outline thickness option shown in Step 6. These are both found under the **Filters > Sketch** category.

149

Artwork

The Graphics panel can be used to add graphical elements to images. This can be done either to existing images or to a blank file, onto which other content can be added. To do this:

1 In the Editor, select **File > New > Blank File** from the Menu bar

2 Access the **Graphics** panel and click on **Backgrounds**

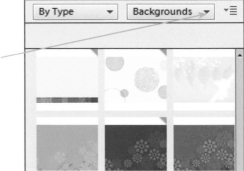

3 Double-click on a background to apply it

4 The background is added to the blank file

5 Repeat Step 2, but select a **Frame** option. This will then enable you to add an image, by clicking here or dragging an open image from the Project Bin

The order in which items appear in the image can be altered by changing the order of the layers in the Layers panel.

6 Repeat Step 2, but select the **Graphics** option to add a graphical element

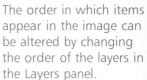

151

7 Repeat Step 2, but select the **Shapes** option to add a 2D shape

If you save the final image as a Photoshop file (.PSD; .PDD) you will still be able to open the image and edit each of the individual elements. However, if you save it as a JPEG, you will not be able to edit any of the artwork elements.

8 Save the final image in the same way as any other file

Depth of Field

Depth of field is a photographic technique where part of a photo is deliberately blurred, for artistic effect. Traditionally, this has been done through camera settings, but in Elements the same effect can be created within the Guided edit mode. To do this:

1 Open the image to which you want to add the depth of field effect

2 Access Guided edit mode. In the **Photo Effects** section, click on the **Depth of Field** button

Photo Effects

Depth Of Field

Guided

3 Click on the **Simple** button

Simple
Add depth in a single step

4 Click on the **Add Blur** button to add a blurred effect to the whole image

1. Add Blur

Click Add Blur button to give the image a default blur.

Click on the **Add Focus Area** button

 Drag on the image, covering the area that you want to appear in focus

Hot tip

The most realistic depth of field effect is done by dragging the **Add Focus Area** tool from front to back, in a straight line. It can also be done diagonally, but this is not something that could easily be achieved with a camera.

Drag this slider to increase the amount of blur of the area that is not in focus

Click on the **Done** button

Line Drawings

By using the Guided edit mode there are a number of artistic special effects that can be applied to images in a straightforward, step-by-step process. One of these is converting images into line drawings. To do this:

 Open the image you want to convert into a line drawing

Don't forget

Other Photo Effects to try are High Key, Low Key, Old Fashioned Photo and Saturated Slide Film Effect.

 Access Guided edit mode. In the **Photo Effects** section, click on the **Line Drawing** button

Photo Effects

Depth Of Field

High Key

Line Drawing

 The process is detailed with each step and a description of what it does. Click on the **Pencil Sketch Effect** button to start the process

1. Pencil Sketch Effect

Click on the button above to give the Image a Pencil Sketch Effect. The effect can be intensified by clicking the button again.

4 Click on the **Adjust Layer Opacity** button to make the lines in the drawing darker

A nice effect can be achieved by bringing back a bit of the original photo's color. Click on the button above to bring back a bit of the original color of the image.

5 Click on the **Levels** button to increase the overall contrast in the image. This can improve the detail in the image

3. Levels

Click on the button above to make the lines in your drawing to be darker.

6 Click on the **Done** button to complete the process

Done

7 The line drawing effect is applied to the image. This can then be saved as a new image

Hot tip

Once a line drawing has been created, and saved, it can then be edited further in Expert edit mode. This can be used to fine-tune the levels, or increase the brightness and contrast.

Photographic Effects

Within the Guided edit mode there are a number of photographic effects that can be added to images. These have been developed by photographers over the years and they are now available within Guided edit mode.

Lomo Camera Effect

This is an effect that puts a vignette around an image and creates a more vibrantly-colored image. To do this:

 Open the image you want to convert into a Lomo Effect

2 Access Guided edit mode. In the **Photo Effects** section, click on the **Lomo Camera Effect** button

3 Click on the next **Lomo Camera Effect** button. This applies the color effect to the image

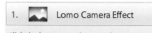

1. Lomo Camera Effect

Click the button to give your image a Lomo camera look. Click the button again to intensify effect.

4 Click on the **Apply Vignette** button. This applies the vignette effect to the whole image. Click on the button again to make the effect more defined

2. Apply Vignette

Add a Vignette to your image to finalize the Lomo camera effect. Click the button again to intensify effect.

5 Click on the **Done** button

Done

Orton Effect

This is another photographic effect that can give a soft-focus appearance to an image. This is also done within the Photo Effects section. To do this, access the Orton Effect button in the same way as for the Lomo Camera Effect:

1 Click on the **Add Orton Effect** button to add the main effect

2 Drag the sliders to edit the effect on the image

3 Click on the **Done** button

Add Orton Effect

Create a soft, dreamy feel for your photo using the Orton Effect, originally created by Michael Orton. Click Add Orton Effect to apply the effect to the photograph.

Blur:
Noise:
Brightness:

Use the slider to manually make changes to the effect.

Don't forget

The Orton Effect was invented by the photographer Michael Orton. It involves overlaying two images of the same subject, with different exposures and one in focus and one out of focus. This results in a soft-focus final image.

Out of Bounds

Another very effective special effect in Elements is called Out of Bounds. This can be used to display a section of an image without the rest of the original photo. This works best when there is one part of the image that obviously sticks out from the rest, such as part of a building, or someone's arm or leg. To create the Out of Bounds effect:

Don't forget

As long as it is a defined area, anything can be used to appear without the rest of the image.

1 Open an image that has an element that will naturally stick out from the rest

2 Access Guided edit mode. In the **Photo Play** section, click on the **Out Of Bounds** button

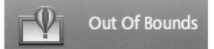

...cont'd

3 Click on the **Add Frame** button

| 1. |  Add Frame |

4 A default frame is added to the image. This can be sized by dragging the buttons situated around the border. It can be moved by clicking on the border and then dragging it into the required position. The area of the frame is the one that will form the main part of the final image

Don't forget

The frame contains the area that will be the main part of the image, not the Out of Bounds selection.

159

5 Hold down **Shift + Ctrl + Alt** to add perspective to the frame. This can be done by dragging the corner buttons and also those in the middle of each side

6 Click on the green arrow to apply the changes to the frame

...cont'd

7 The frame is displayed, with the rest of the image grayed-out

8 Click on the **Selection Tool** button

2.	🔍	Selection Tool

9 Drag over the area that will appear outside the main image

Hot tip

Zoom in on the area to be selected so that you can do this with greater precision and accuracy.

Click on the **Out of Bounds Effect** button

3. Out of Bounds Effect

 The area selected in Step 9 now appears on its own, outside the area created by the frame

 Click on the **Add Background Gradient** button to add a background gradient to the final image

4. Add Background Gradient
Add a Gradient Background to enhance the effect.

5. Add Shadow:

Small   Medium   Large

Add depth to your image by selecting an appropriate shadow size.

 Click on one of the **Add Shadow** buttons to add a drop shadow to the image

 **Don't forget**

Another Photo Play option is Picture Stack, which creates a broken-up version of a single photo. It can be broken into 4, 8 or 12 separate pieces.

 Click on the **Done** button to complete the process

Done

161

Pop Art

One of the best known artistic techniques is pop art, made famous by Andy Warhol in the 1960s. Now, it is possible to create your own pop art images with Elements. To do this:

 Open the image you want to convert to pop art

 Access Guided edit mode. In the **Photo Play** section, click on the **Pop Art** button

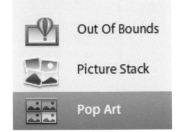
Select a style for your pop art creation

 Click on the **Convert Image Mode** button

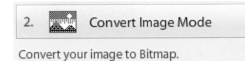

5 Click on the **Add Color** button

Add a Color fill adjustment layer.

6 The image is converted into a single pop art image

Don't forget

The colors for the Pop Art effect are created automatically when the effect is applied.

7 Click on the **Duplicate Image** button

Duplicate image with different pop colors.

8 The image is converted into the iconic pop art style, with four differently-colored versions of the same image

9 Click on the **Done** button to complete the process

Done

Reflections

Reflections of an image can be one of the most satisfying photographic effects. Images reflected in water, or on a clear surface, can create a very artistic and calming effect. However, it can be difficult to get the perfect reflection when taking an original photo. To help overcome this Elements has a Guided edit that can create the effect for you. To do this:

Beware

If you select an image that does not have enough detail in the foreground, the join with the reflected image may appear too severe and slightly unnatural.

164

1 Open the image you want to use for the reflection. If possible, use one with some objects in the foreground

2 Access Guided edit mode. In the **Photo Play** section, click on the **Reflection** button

Photo Play

Out Of Bounds

Picture Stack

Pop Art

Reflection

3 Click on the **Add Reflection** button

1. Add Reflection

Add a reflection to your image by clicking the Add Reflection button.

4 The reflection effect is applied to the image

5 Depending on the type of reflection you are creating you can add a background color by selecting the **Eyedropper Tool** button and clicking on the **Fill Background** button

2. Eyedropper tool

Use the Eyedropper tool to choose a background color for your reflection.

3. Fill Background

Fill the background with your selected color.

Beware

If a background color is used, this will be applied to the reflected image. However, this step does not have to be used.

6 Select the type of reflection effect you want to create

4. Apply an effect to make your reflection more realistic.

Floor   Glass   Water

...cont'd

7 Each option has different dialog boxes which can be used to set the amount. Click on the **OK** button to apply the selected effect

Don't forget

When an effect is applied, it looks more defined the more that you zoom in on an image. To see it in its normal state it is best to view the image at 1:1, i.e. 100%.

8 The effect is applied to the reflected half of the image

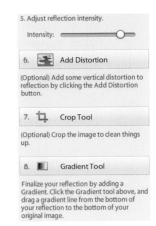

9 Additional options can be applied to fine-tune the selected effect further

10 Click on the **Done** button to complete the process

Done

10 Sharing and Creating

This chapter shows how you can share images creatively and also use and edit them in artistic projects.

Saving Images for the Web

One of the issues for images that are going to be shared online is file size. This must be small enough so that the images can be downloaded quickly on a web page, or as an attachment in an email. To assist in this, Elements has a function for saving images in different formats and also altering the quality settings for each format. This enables you to balance the quality and file size, so that you have the optimum image for use online. To do this:

Don't forget

Preparing images for the Web is also known as optimizing.

1 Open an image in any of the Editor modes and select **File > Save for Web** from the Menu bar

2 The original image is shown on the left of the **Save for Web** window

3 Select options for optimizing the image here

4 The preview of the optimized image is shown here, once the settings have been applied

...cont'd

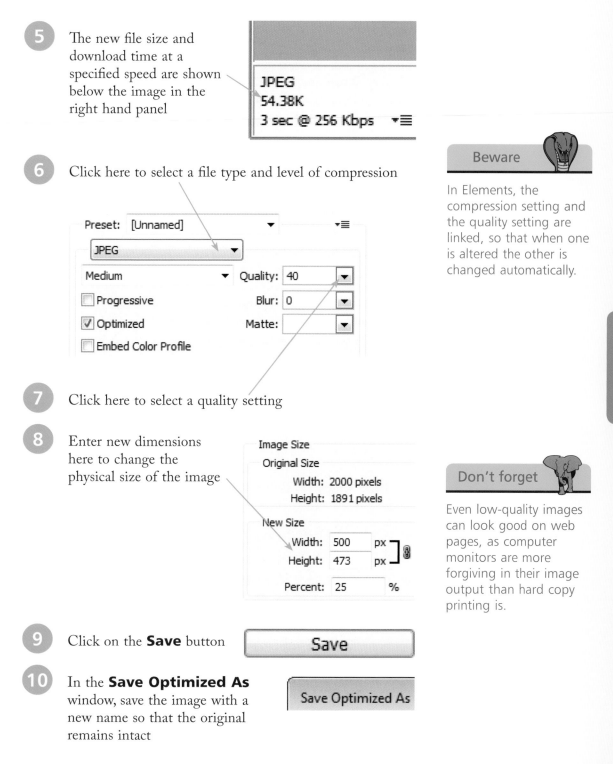

5 The new file size and download time at a specified speed are shown below the image in the right hand panel

JPEG
54.38K
3 sec @ 256 Kbps

6 Click here to select a file type and level of compression

Preset: [Unnamed]

JPEG

Medium — Quality: 40

☐ Progressive — Blur: 0

☑ Optimized — Matte:

☐ Embed Color Profile

7 Click here to select a quality setting

8 Enter new dimensions here to change the physical size of the image

Image Size
Original Size
 Width: 2000 pixels
 Height: 1891 pixels

New Size
 Width: 500 px
 Height: 473 px
 Percent: 25 %

9 Click on the **Save** button

Save

10 In the **Save Optimized As** window, save the image with a new name so that the original remains intact

Save Optimized As

Beware

In Elements, the compression setting and the quality setting are linked, so that when one is altered the other is changed automatically.

169

Don't forget

Even low-quality images can look good on web pages, as computer monitors are more forgiving in their image output than hard copy printing is.

About Share Mode

Share mode enables you to output your images in a variety of ways, and also send them to friends and family in different formats. Some of these involve third-party services and these will vary depending on your own location. Also, some of the options offered through the Share mode require the video-editing program, Elements Premiere. The standard options within Share mode are:

- **Share to Flickr and Facebook.** This can be used to share images to these popular social media sites

- **Email Attachments.** This can be used to attach photos to emails via your email program

- **Photo Mail.** This can be used to produce creative email messages with your photos

- **Vimeo.** This is an online video-sharing service, where your Elements videos can be shared and viewed

- **YouTube.** This can be used to upload videos to YouTube

- **Video to Photoshop Showcase.** This can be used to share any video clips you have in Elements

- **Online Album.** This can be used to display your photos online, using the available third-party suppliers

- **Burn Video DVD/BluRay.** This requires Elements Premiere

- **Online Video Sharing.** This requires Elements Premiere

- **Mobile Phones.** This requires Elements Premiere

- **PDF SlideShow.** This creates a slide show in PDF format which means that it should be possible to open it on most computers

- **Adobe Revel.** This is an app that can be used to share your photos. Elements can share photos directly with Adobe Revel

Don't forget

The Adobe Revel app is currently available for Mac computers, iPads and iPhones and can be downloaded from the Mac App Store. There are also versions planned for Android and Windows devices, although there is presently an importer available for Android. For full details visit the Revel website at *www.adoberevel.com*

f	Facebook
@	Email Attachments
✉	Photo Mail
Vimeo	Vimeo
YouTube	YouTube
◎	Video to Photoshop Showcase
••	Flickr
▣	Online Album
◉	Burn Video DVD / BluRay
▦	Online Video Sharing
📱	Mobile Phones
PDF	PDF Slide Show
◑	Adobe Revel

To use Share mode

1 In either the Editor or the Organizer, click on the **Share** tab and select an option

2 Add content to be shared (either by selecting it initially or by dragging it into the content panel)

Don't forget

Each Share option has a slightly different wizard, but the basic process is the same for each one.

171

3 Some of the Share options require a form of registration for the selected option

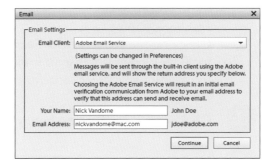

4 Format the content using the wizards and templates within the Share section. Click on the **Next** button to move through the wizards and templates. Click on the **Done** button to complete the process and share your photos with the selected Share option

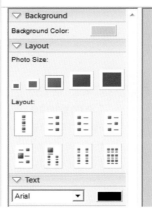

Sharing on Facebook

With the explosion in popularity of social networking sites such as Facebook, it's no surprise that there are now a number of applications available for people to upload photos to their own pages on these sites. Within Elements it is now possible to upload photos directly to Facebook. To do this:

1 Select a photo in the Organizer. Select the **Share** option and click on the **Facebook** button

Don't forget

Images can also be shared on the photo-sharing site Flickr. The process is similar to the one here for sharing on Facebook.

2 You will be asked to authorize your account so that Elements can become an approved method for uploading your Facebook photos. Check on the **Download Facebook friend list** to allow Elements to use your Facebook friends for face recognition when searching for images

3 Click on the **Authorize** button

4 Log in to your Facebook account, or create a new one

5 Click on the **Complete Authorization** button to allow Elements to be an uploader for your Facebook photos

About Create Mode

Image-editing programs have now evolved to a point where there is almost as much emphasis on using images creatively as there is on editing them. Elements has an excellent range of options for displaying your images in some stunningly creative ways, called, appropriately enough, Create mode. These can be saved in the Organizer for viewing or sharing. The standard options within Create mode are:

- **Photo Prints.** This can be used to print photos locally on your own printer, or using an online service

- **Photo Book.** This creates a selection of formatted images that can be printed in a presentational book

- **Greeting Cards.** This creates your own personalized cards

- **Photo Calendar.** This creates your own personalized calendars

- **Photo Collage.** This can be used to assemble several images

- **Slide Show.** This creates a slide show of selected images

- **Instant Movie.** This requires Elements Premiere

- **DVD with Menu.** This requires Elements Premiere and can be used to create a DVD of your photos and videos

- **CD and DVD Jacket.** This can be used to create customized CD and DVD covers

- **CD and DVD Label.** This can be used to create customized CD and DVD labels

To use Create mode:

1. In either the Editor or the Organizer, click on the **Create** button

2. Select one of the Create options

Hot tip

To only view Create projects in the Organizer, select **Find > By Media Type > Projects** from the Organizer Menu bar.

Don't forget

The Instant Movie and DVD with Menu options are only available from within the Organizer.

Don't forget

In Create mode, Pages, Layouts and Graphics buttons are added to the standard Taskbar.

...cont'd

 In the dialog window for the Create option select a size at which the creation will be printed

Sizes
Print locally
297.00 x 210.00 mm
300.00 x 300.00 mm

4 Select a theme for the creation (this will be applied across the whole creation, even if it has multiple pages). If there is a blue arrow in the top right-hand corner this indicates that this is an online resource which will be downloaded before use

174

5 A preview of the layout for the creation is shown in the right-hand panel

6 Click on the **OK** button

7 If the theme is an online resource (see Step 4) this will be downloaded to Elements

Adobe Photoshop Elements

Downloading Asset. Please wait..

Cancel

8 The creation project document is created

Title Here
Your Text Here

9 Click on these arrows to move between the pages of the creation

‹ **Title Page** ›

10 Drag this slider to increase and decrease the viewing size of the creation

Zoom: ——○—— 97%

Don't forget

Text blocks can be used to add your own messages to your photos within creations.

11 Click on a text block and overtype to create your own text

Beautiful Bulgaria
Your Text Here

12 Click on the **Pages** button on the Taskbar and click here to add new pages to the creation

Pages

Create

Title Page

1   2

...cont'd

 Click on the **Layouts** button on the Taskbar and select a layout for the way the photos in the creation will appear

 Add more photos to the layout by dragging them onto the one of the image placeholders or by clicking on it and selecting a photo

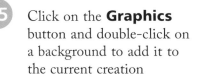

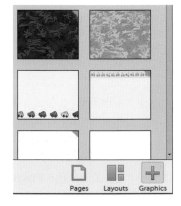

 Click on the **Graphics** button and double-click on a background to add it to the current creation

 Click on the **Save** button to complete the creation. It will then still need to be saved within Elements

Save

Once a project has

been saved it is displayed in the Organizer. This means that it can then be opened again and edited if required

Editing Creations

By default, Creations are produced using wizards and templates within the Create area. This makes it straightforward in terms of producing Creations, but without the power of Expert edit mode. However, in Elements you can now select an Advanced mode so that you can use all of the standard editing tools on the parts of your creation. To do this:

1 In Create mode, there are limited independent editing options. The editing is done within the Create section

2 Click on the **Advanced Mode** button

Advanced Mode

3 The full Expert edit mode Toolbox becomes available and these tools can be used to edit the creation

Don't forget

When an item is edited within Advanced Mode, this is done independently of the other elements of the creation, which remain untouched.

...cont'd

④ Click on the **Layers** button on the Taskbar

Layers

⑤ The Layers panel allows you to examine the structure of the creation. Each layer can now be edited separately

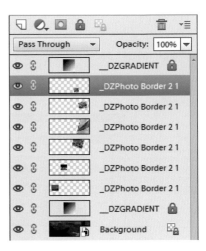

⑥ If you want to edit a specific item within Advanced mode, you will be alerted to the fact that the item will need to be simplified, which reduces the independence of the item compared to the rest of the image. Click on the **OK** button to continue

Adobe Photoshop Elements 11

⚠ You are trying to edit a photo in a frame layer but first it must be simplified. You will lose resolution independence. Do you want to continue?

OK   Cancel

⑦ Click on the **Basic Mode** button to return to the regular Create mode

Basic Mode

⑧ A project file is denoted by this icon in the top right-hand corner

11 Printing Images

This chapter shows how to size images for printing, and how to print them in a variety of formats.

Print Size

Before you start printing images in Elements, it is important to ensure that they are going to be produced at the required size. Since the pixels within an image are not a set size, the printed dimensions of an image can be altered according to your needs. This is done by specifying how many pixels are used within each inch of the image. The more pixels per inch (PPI) then the higher the quality of the printed image, but the smaller in size it will be.

To set the print size of an image (in any of the Editor modes):

1 Open an image and select **Image > Resize> Image Size** from the Menu bar

2 Uncheck the **Resample Image** box. This will ensure that the physical image size, i.e. the number of pixels in the image, remains unchanged when the resolution is changed

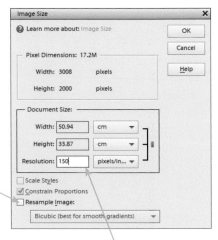

3 The current resolution and document size (print size) are displayed here

4 Enter a new figure in the Resolution box (here, the resolution has been increased from 150 to 300). This affects the Document size, i.e. the size at which the image prints

Document Size:

Width: 25.47 cm

Height: 16.93 cm

Resolution: 300 pixels/in...

Print Functions

The Print functions in Elements can be accessed from the Menu bar in either the Editor or the Organizer, by selecting **File > Print**. Also, all of the print functions can be selected from Create mode. To print to your local printer using this method:

1 Select an image in either the Editor or the Organizer, click on the **Create** button and click on the **Photo Prints** button

2 Click on the **Local Printer** button

3 The main print window displays the default option for how the printed image will appear and also options for changing the properties of the print

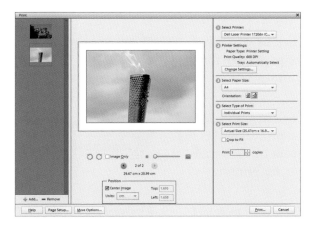

Don't forget

The currently-active images are shown in the left-hand panel of the Print window.

4 Click the **Add** button to include more images in the current print job, or select an image and click on the **Remove** button to exclude it

...cont'd

5 Use these options to rotate an image for printing, change its size, or position

Hot tip

Check on the **Center Image** box in Step 5 to have the image printed in the center of the page.

Image Only		2 of 2	

29.67 cm x 20.99 cm

Position
☑ Center Image   Top: 1.693
Units: cm ▼   Left: 1.658

6 Click here to select a destination printer to which you want to send your print

1 Select Printer:
Dell Laser Printer 1720dn (C... ▼

7 Click on the **Change Settings** button to change the properties for your own local printer

2 Printer Settings:
   Paper Type: Printer Setting
   Print Quality: 600 DPI
   Tray: Automatically Select
   Change Settings...

8 Click here to select the paper size for printing

3 Select Paper Size:
A4 ▼
Orientation: 🔲 🔲

9 Click here to select the print type, i.e. the layout of the image you are printing

4 Select Type of Print:
Individual Prints ▼

10 Click here to select the size at which you want your image to be printed

5 Select Print Size:
Actual Size (25.47cm x 16.9... ▼
☐ Crop to Fit

11 Click on the **Print** button to print your image with the settings selected above

Print...

Print Layouts

Rather than just offering the sole function of printing a single image on a sheet of paper, Elements has two options that can be used when printing images, which can help reduce the number of sheets of paper used.

Picture Package

This can be used to print out copies of different images on a single piece of paper. To do this:

1 Select an image in either the Editor or the Organizer, click on the Create button and click on the **Picture Package** button

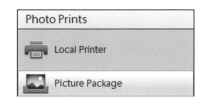

2 The layout for the Picture Package is displayed in the main print window

3 Under **Select a Layout**, select how many images you want on a page and, if required, select a type of frame for the printed images

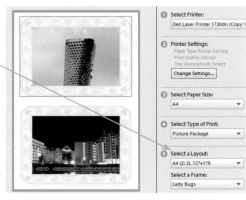

Hot tip

When buying a printer, choose one that has borderless printing. This means that it can print to the very edge of the page. This is particularly useful for items, such as files, produced as a Picture Package.

Don't forget

The Picture Package function is useful for printing images in a combination of sizes, such as for family portraits.

...cont'd

Contact Sheets

This can be used to create and print thumbnail versions of a large number of images. To do this:

1 Select an image in either the Editor or the Organizer, click on the Create button and click on the **Contact Sheet** button

Don't forget

When a contact sheet is created, new thumbnail images are generated. The original images are unaffected.

2 The layout for the Contact Sheet is displayed in the main Print window

3 Click under **Select Type of Print** and select the number of columns to be displayed on the contact sheet

Online Prints

Printing digital images online is now firmly established and is is an excellent way of getting high quality, economical, prints without leaving the comfort of your own home:

1 Open an image, or images, in either the Editor, or select them in the Organizer. Click on the **Create** button and select Photo Prints. There

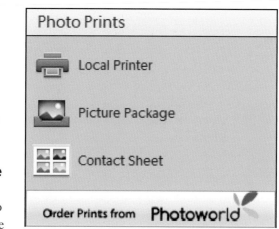

are options for printing images on your own printer, and also services for online prints. These will be specific to your own location

2 When you click on one of the services you will be taken to its website, from where you will be able to order your online prints. You will have to register for the site initially, which will be free. Most services will also have an option for uploading your photos, so that they can also be viewed and shared online

Hot tip

When printing images, either online or on your own printer, make sure that they have been captured at the highest resolution setting on your camera, to ensure the best printed quality.

185

Creating PDF Files

PDF (Portable Document Format) is a file format that is used to maintain the original formatting and style of a document, so that it can be viewed on a variety of different devices and types of computers. In general, it is usually used for documents that contain text and images, such as information pamphlets, magazine features and chapters from books. However, image files, such as JPEGs, can also be converted into PDF and this can be done within Elements without the need for any other special software. To do this:

Don't forget

PDF files are an excellent way to share files so that other people can print them. All that is required is a copy of Adobe Acrobat Reader, which is bundled with most software packages on computers, or can be downloaded from the Adobe website at: *www.adobe.com*

1 Open an image and select **File > Save As** from the Menu bar

2 Select a destination folder and make sure the format is set to Photoshop PDF. Then click **Save**

3 The PDF file is created and can be opened in Adobe Acrobat or Elements

Index